MznLnx

Missing Links Exam Preps

Exam Prep for

Health Care Administration: Planning, Implementing, and Managing Organized Delivery Systems

Wolper, 4th Edition

The MznLnx Exam Prep is your link from the texbook and lecture to your exams.
The MznLnx Exam Preps are unauthorized and comprehensive reviews of your textbooks.

All material provided by MznLnx and Rico Publications (c) 2010
Textbook publishers and textbook authors do not particpate in or contribute to these reviews.

MznLnx

Rico Publications

Exam Prep for Health Care Administration: Planning, Implementing, and Managing Organized Delivery Systems
4th Edition
Wolper

Publisher: Raymond Houge
Assistant Editor: Michael Rouger
Text and Cover Designer: Lisa Buckner
Marketing Manager: Sara Swagger
Project Manager, Editorial Production: Jerry Emerson
Art Director: Vernon Lowerui

Product Manager: Dave Mason
Editorial Assitant: Rachel Guzmanji
Pedagogy: Debra Long
Cover Image: Jim Reed/Getty Images
Text and Cover Printer: City Printing, Inc.
Compositor: Media Mix, Inc.

(c) 2010 Rico Publications
ALL RIGHTS RESERVED. No part of this work covered by the copyright may be reproduced or used in any form or by an means--graphic, electronic, or mechanical, including photocopying, recording, taping, Web distribution, information storage, and retrieval systems, or in any other manner--without the written permission of the publisher.

Printed in the United States
ISBN:

For more information about our products, contact us at:

Dave.Mason@RicoPublications.com

For permission to use material from this text or

product, submit a request online to:

Dave.Mason@RicoPublications.com

Contents

CHAPTER 1
International Health Care: A 12-Country Comparison 1
CHAPTER 2
Organized Delivery Systems 4
CHAPTER 3
Legal Implications of Business Arrangements in the Healthcare Industry 11
CHAPTER 4
Stakeholder Management—Strategies and Styles 16
CHAPTER 5
Financial Management of Organized Health Care Delivery Systems 20
CHAPTER 6
Human Resources Management in Organized Delivery Systems 34
CHAPTER 7
Labor and Employment Laws Applicable to Organized Delivery Systems 44
CHAPTER 8
The Management of Nursing Services 54
CHAPTER 9
Planning Healthcare Facilities and Managing the Development Process 56
CHAPTER 10
Financing of Healthcare Facilities 59
CHAPTER 11
Marketing Healthcare Services 64
CHAPTER 12
Health Care Information Systems: An Organized Delivery System Perspective 68
CHAPTER 13
Management Engineering 70
CHAPTER 14
Ambulatory Care 74
CHAPTER 15
Managed Health Care 76
CHAPTER 16
Ethical Considerations in the Provision of Healthcare Services 81
CHAPTER 17
Bioterrorism Preparedness 83
CHAPTER 18
The History of Hospitals 84
CHAPTER 19
Hospital Organization and Management 86
CHAPTER 20
Patient Access Services: Into, Through, and Out of the Healthcare Process 89

Contents (Cont.)

CHAPTER 21
Laboratories 91

CHAPTER 22
Pharmacy 94

CHAPTER 23
Material and Resource Management 98

CHAPTER 24
Designing and Implementing a Hospital Compliance Program 101

CHAPTER 25
Quality Assurance and Improvement 104

CHAPTER 26
Physician Practice: Organization and Operation 108

CHAPTER 27
Implementing a Physician Practice Compliance Program 110

ANSWER KEY 114

TO THE STUDENT

COMPREHENSIVE

The *MznLnx* Exam Prep series is designed to help you pass your exams. Editors at MznLnx review your textbooks and then prepare these practice exams to help you master the textbook material. Unlike study guides, workbooks, and practice tests provided by the texbook publisher and textbook authors, *MznLnx* gives you **all** of the material in each chapter in exam form, not just samples, so you can be sure to nail your exam.

MECHANICAL

The MznLnx Exam Prep series creates exams that will help you learn the subject matter as well as test you on your understanding. Each question is designed to help you master the concept. Just working through the exams, you gain an understanding of the subject--its a simple mechanical process that produces success.

INTEGRATED STUDY GUIDE AND REVIEW

MznLnx is not just a set of exams designed to test you, its also a comprehensive review of the subject content. Each exam question is also a review of the concept, making sure that you will get the answer correct without having to go to other sources of material. You learn as you go! Its the easiest way to pass an exam.

HUMOR

Studying can be tedious and dry. MznLnx's instructional design includes moderate humor within the exam questions on occassion, to break the tedium and revitalize the brain

Chapter 1. International Health Care: A 12-Country Comparison

1. _____ is the activity that the selling organization undertakes to reduce customer account defections. The success of this activity is when the customer account places an additional order before a 12-month period has expired. Note that ideally these orders will need to contribute similar financial amounts to the previous 12 months.

   a. Foreign ownership
   b. Customer retention
   c. Process automation
   d. Business rule

2. _____ or _____ data refers to selected population characteristics as used in government, marketing or opinion research, or the _____ profiles used in such research. Note the distinction from the term 'demography' Commonly-used _____s include race, age, income, disabilities, mobility (in terms of travel time to work or number of vehicles available), educational attainment, home ownership, employment status, and even location.

   a. Affiliation
   b. Adam Smith
   c. Abraham Harold Maslow
   d. Demographic

3. _____ means how much each individual receives, in monetary terms, of the yearly income generated in the country. This is what each citizen is to receive if the yearly national income is divided equally among everyone. _____ is usually reported in units of currency per year.

   a. 1990 Clean Air Act
   b. Per capita income
   c. 33 Strategies of War
   d. 28-hour day

4. In economics, business, retail, and accounting, a _____ is the value of money that has been used up to produce something, and hence is not available for use anymore. In economics, a _____ is an alternative that is given up as a result of a decision. In business, the _____ may be one of acquisition, in which case the amount of money expended to acquire it is counted as _____.

   a. Cost overrun
   b. Fixed costs
   c. Cost allocation
   d. Cost

5. The _____ or gross domestic income (GDI), a basic measure of an economy's economic performance, is the market value of all final goods and services made within the borders of a nation in a year. _____ can be defined in three ways, all of which are conceptually identical. First, it is equal to the total expenditures for all final goods and services produced within the country in a stipulated period of time (usually a 365-day year).

   a. Productivity management
   b. Human capital
   c. Perfect competition
   d. Gross domestic product

6. _____ is an advertisement in which a particular product specifically mentions a competitor by name for the express purpose of showing why the competitor is inferior to the product naming it.

This should not be confused with parody advertisements, where a fictional product is being advertised for the purpose of poking fun at the particular advertisement, nor should it be confused with the use of a coined brand name for the purpose of comparing the product without actually naming an actual competitor. ('Wikipedia tastes better and is less filling than the Encyclopedia Galactica.')

In the 1980s, during what has been referred to as the cola wars, soft-drink manufacturer Pepsi ran a series of advertisements where people, caught on hidden camera, in a blind taste test, chose Pepsi over rival Coca-Cola.

   a. 28-hour day
   b. 33 Strategies of War
   c. Comparative advertising
   d. 1990 Clean Air Act

7. In game theory, an _____ is a set of moves or strategies taken by the players, or their payoffs resulting from the actions or strategies taken by all players. The two are complementary in that given knowledge of the set of strategies of all players, the final state of the game is known, as are any relevant payoffs. In a game where chance or a random event is involved, the _____ is not known from only the set of strategies, but is only realized when the random event(s) are realized.
   a. Outcome
   b. AAAI
   c. A Stake in the Outcome
   d. A4e

8. _____ of the learning curve effect and the closely related experience curve effect express the relationship between equations for experience and efficiency or between efficiency gains and investment in the effort. The experience of 'learning curves' was first observed by the 19th Century German psychologist Hermann Ebbinghaus according to the difficulty of memorizing varying numbers of verbal stimuli, and subsequent learning about the complex processes of learning are discussed in the

.

The rule used for representing the learning curve effect states that the more times a task has been performed, the less time will be required on each subsequent iteration.

   a. Spatial Decision Support Systems
   b. Distribution
   c. Models
   d. Point biserial correlation coefficient

9. In probability theory, a probability distribution is called _____ if its cumulative distribution function is _____. This is equivalent to saying that for random variables X with the distribution in question, Pr[X = a] = 0 for all real numbers a, i.e.: the probability that X attains the value a is zero, for any number a. If the distribution of X is _____ then X is called a _____ random variable.
   a. Connectionist expert systems
   b. Decision tree pruning
   c. Continuous
   d. Pay Band

10. Quality management can be considered to have three main components: quality control, quality assurance and _____. Quality management is focused not only on product quality, but also the means to achieve it. Quality management therefore uses quality assurance and control of processes as well as products to achieve more consistent quality.
    a. 1990 Clean Air Act
    b. 28-hour day
    c. Quality improvement
    d. Quality management

11. A chief executive officer (_____) or chief executive is one of the highest-ranking corporate officer (executive) or administrator in charge of total management. An individual selected as President and _____ of a corporation, company, organization, or agency, reports to the board of directors. In internal communication and press releases, many companies capitalize the term and those of other high positions, even when they are not proper nouns.
    a. Chief executive officer
    b. Director of communications
    c. Portfolio manager
    d. CEO

12. A _____ is defined as someone who controls access to something. It also refers to individuals who decide whether a given message will be distributed by a mass medium.

_____s serve several different purposes such as academic admissions, financial advising, and news editing.

a. 33 Strategies of War
b. 28-hour day
c. 1990 Clean Air Act
d. Gatekeeper

13. _____ refers to planned and systematic production processes that provide confidence in a product's suitability for its intended purpose. Refer to the definition by Merriam-Webster for further information. It is a set of activities intended to ensure that products (goods and/or services) satisfy customer requirements in a systematic, reliable fashion.

a. 1990 Clean Air Act
b. 28-hour day
c. Risk assessment
d. Quality Assurance

Chapter 2. Organized Delivery Systems

1. _____ is a broad label that refers to any individuals or households that use goods and services generated within the economy. The concept of a _____ is used in different contexts, so that the usage and significance of the term may vary.

Typically when business people and economists talk of _____s they are talking about person as _____, an aggregated commodity item with little individuality other than that expressed in the buy/not-buy decision.

- a. 33 Strategies of War
- b. 28-hour day
- c. 1990 Clean Air Act
- d. Consumer

2. _____ is an advertisement in which a particular product specifically mentions a competitor by name for the express purpose of showing why the competitor is inferior to the product naming it.

This should not be confused with parody advertisements, where a fictional product is being advertised for the purpose of poking fun at the particular advertisement, nor should it be confused with the use of a coined brand name for the purpose of comparing the product without actually naming an actual competitor. ('Wikipedia tastes better and is less filling than the Encyclopedia Galactica.')

In the 1980s, during what has been referred to as the cola wars, soft-drink manufacturer Pepsi ran a series of advertisements where people, caught on hidden camera, in a blind taste test, chose Pepsi over rival Coca-Cola.

- a. 28-hour day
- b. 1990 Clean Air Act
- c. 33 Strategies of War
- d. Comparative advertising

3. _____, known in the United States as antitrust law, has three main elements:

- prohibiting agreements or practices that restrict free trading and competition between business entities. This includes in particular the repression of cartels.
- banning abusive behavior by a firm dominating a market, or anti-competitive practices that tend to lead to such a dominant position. Practices controlled in this way may include predatory pricing, tying, price gouging, refusal to deal, and many others.
- supervising the mergers and acquisitions of large corporations, including some joint ventures. Transactions that are considered to threaten the competitive process can be prohibited altogether, or approved subject to 'remedies' such as an obligation to divest part of the merged business or to offer licenses or access to facilities to enable other businesses to continue competing.

The substance and practice of _____ varies from jurisdiction to jurisdiction. Protecting the interests of consumers (consumer welfare) and ensuring that entrepreneurs have an opportunity to compete in the market economy are often treated as important objectives. _____ is closely connected with law on deregulation of access to markets, state aids and subsidies, the privatization of state owned assets and the establishment of independent sector regulators. In recent decades, _____ has been viewed as a way to provide better public services.

a. Rulemaking
b. Competition law
c. Federal Employers Liability Act
d. Right to Financial Privacy Act

4. _____ consists of the mental process of thinking involved with the process of judging the merits of multiple options and selecting one of them for action. Some simple examples include deciding whether to get up in the morning or go back to sleep, or selecting a given route for a journey. More complex examples (often decisions that affect what a person thinks or their core beliefs) include choosing a lifestyle, religious affiliation, or political position.
   a. Choice
   b. Championship mobilization
   c. Trade study
   d. Groups decision making

5. In microeconomics and strategic management, the term _____ describes a type of ownership and control. It is a strategy used by a business or corporation that seeks to sell a type of product in numerous markets. _____ in marketing is much more common than vertical integration is in production.
   a. Horizontal Integration
   b. Career development
   c. No-bid contract
   d. Farmshoring

6. A _____ is one of several ways of doing research whether it is social science related or even socially related. It is an intensive study of a single group, incident, or community.Other ways include experiments, surveys, multiple histories, and analysis of archival information .

Rather than using samples and following a rigid protocol to examine limited number of variables, _____ methods involve an in-depth, longitudinal examination of a single instance or event: a case.

   a. Standard operating procedure
   b. Case study
   c. 1990 Clean Air Act
   d. Longitudinal study

7. _____ refers to the movement of cash into or out of a business or financial product. It is usually measured during a specified, finite period of time. Measurement of _____ can be used

   - to determine a project's rate of return or value. The time of _____s into and out of projects are used as inputs in financial models such as internal rate of return, and net present value.
   - to determine problems with a business's liquidity. Being profitable does not necessarily mean being liquid. A company can fail because of a shortage of cash, even while profitable.
   - as an alternate measure of a business's profits when it is believed that accrual accounting concepts do not represent economic realities. For example, a company may be notionally profitable but generating little operational cash (as may be the case for a company that barters its products rather than selling for cash.) In such a case, the company may be deriving additional operating cash by issuing shares evaluating default risk, re-investment requirements, etc.

_____ is a generic term used differently depending on the context. It may be defined by users for their own purposes.

   a. Gross profit margin
   b. Sweat equity
   c. Gross profit
   d. Cash flow

Chapter 2. Organized Delivery Systems

8. _____ is one of the managerial functions like planning, organizing, staffing and directing. It is an important function because it helps to check the errors and to take the corrective action so that deviation from standards are minimized and stated goals of the organization are achieved in desired manner. According to modern concepts, _____ is a foreseeing action whereas earlier concept of _____ was used only when errors were detected. _____ in management means setting standards, measuring actual performance and taking corrective action.
   a. Decision tree pruning
   b. Schedule of reinforcement
   c. Turnover
   d. Control

9. _____ generally refers to a list of all planned expenses and revenues. It is a plan for saving and spending. A _____ is an important concept in microeconomics, which uses a _____ line to illustrate the trade-offs between two or more goods.
   a. 33 Strategies of War
   b. 28-hour day
   c. Budget
   d. 1990 Clean Air Act

10. A mutual shareholder or _____ is an individual or company (including a corporation) that legally owns one or more shares of stock in a joint stock company. A company's shareholders collectively own that company. Thus, the typical goal of such companies is to enhance shareholder value.
    a. Free riding
    b. 1990 Clean Air Act
    c. Stockholder
    d. Shareholder

11. In business, _____, operating income margin, operating profit margin or return on sales (ROS) is the ratio of operating income (operating profit in the UK) divided by net sales, usually presented in percent.

$$\text{Operating margin} = \left(\frac{\text{Operating income}}{\text{Revenue}}\right)$$

(Relevant figures in italics)

$$\text{Operating margin} = \left(\frac{6,318}{24,088}\right) = \underline{\underline{26.23\%}}$$

It is a measurement of what proportion of a company's revenue is left over, before taxes and other indirect costs (such as rent, bonus, interest, etc.), after paying for variable costs of production as wages, raw materials, etc. A good _____ is needed for a company to be able to pay for its fixed costs, such as interest on debt.

   a. AAAI
   b. Operating margin
   c. A Stake in the Outcome
   d. A4e

12. In microeconomics and management, the term _____ describes a style of management control. Vertically integrated companies are united through a hierarchy with a common owner. Usually each member of the hierarchy produces a different product or (market-specific) service, and the products combine to satisfy a common need.
    a. 33 Strategies of War
    b. 28-hour day
    c. 1990 Clean Air Act
    d. Vertical integration

Chapter 2. Organized Delivery Systems

13. _____ or _____ data refers to selected population characteristics as used in government, marketing or opinion research, or the _____ profiles used in such research. Note the distinction from the term 'demography' Commonly-used _____s include race, age, income, disabilities, mobility (in terms of travel time to work or number of vehicles available), educational attainment, home ownership, employment status, and even location.
   a. Adam Smith
   b. Abraham Harold Maslow
   c. Affiliation
   d. Demographic

14. A _____ or chief executive is one of the highest-ranking corporate officer (executive) or administrator in charge of total management. An individual selected as President and _____ of a corporation, company, organization, or agency, reports to the board of directors. In internal communication and press releases, many companies capitalize the term and those of other high positions, even when they are not proper nouns.
   a. Financial analyst
   b. Chief brand officer
   c. Purchasing manager
   d. Chief executive officer

15. _____ analysis (CEA) is a form of economic analysis that compares the relative expenditure (costs) and outcomes (effects) of two or more courses of action. _____ analysis is often used where a full cost-benefit analysis is inappropriate e.g. the problem is to determine how best to comply with a legal requirement. Typically the CEA is expressed in terms of a ratio where the denominator is a gain in health from a measure (years of life, premature births averted, sight-years gained) and the numerator is the cost of the health gain.
   a. Cost-effectiveness
   b. Financial risk
   c. Frisch elasticity
   d. Choquet integral

16. While _____ literally refers to a person responsible for the performance of duties involved in running an organization, the exact meaning of the role is variable, depending on the organization.

While there is no clear line between executive or principal and inferior officers, principal officers are high-level officials in the executive branch of U.S. government such as department heads of independent agencies. In Humphrey's Executor v. United States, 295 U.S. 602 (1935), the Court distinguished between _____s and quasi-legislative or quasi-judicial officers by stating that the former serve at the pleasure of the President and may be removed at his discretion.

   a. Unreported employment
   b. Easement
   c. Australian Fair Pay and Conditions Standard
   d. Executive officer

17. _____ of the learning curve effect and the closely related experience curve effect express the relationship between equations for experience and efficiency or between efficiency gains and investment in the effort. The experience of 'learning curves' was first observed by the 19th Century German psychologist Hermann Ebbinghaus according to the difficulty of memorizing varying numbers of verbal stimuli, and subsequent learning about the complex processes of learning are discussed in the

The rule used for representing the learning curve effect states that the more times a task has been performed, the less time will be required on each subsequent iteration.

Chapter 2. Organized Delivery Systems

    a. Point biserial correlation coefficient
    b. Spatial Decision Support Systems
    c. Distribution
    d. Models

18. In economics, business, retail, and accounting, a _____ is the value of money that has been used up to produce something, and hence is not available for use anymore. In economics, a _____ is an alternative that is given up as a result of a decision. In business, the _____ may be one of acquisition, in which case the amount of money expended to acquire it is counted as _____.
    a. Fixed costs
    b. Cost overrun
    c. Cost allocation
    d. Cost

19. _____ is the amount of goods and services that a labourer produces in a given amount of time. It is one of several types of productivity that economists measure. _____ can be measured for a firm, a process or a country.
    a. Retroactive overtime
    b. Business Network Transformation
    c. Time and attendance
    d. Labour productivity

20. _____ refers to metrics and measures of output from production processes, per unit of input. Labor _____, for example, is typically measured as a ratio of output per labor-hour, an input. _____ may be conceived of as a metrics of the technical or engineering efficiency of production.
    a. Productivity
    b. Value engineering
    c. Master production schedule
    d. Remanufacturing

21. _____ is an increasingly broadening term with which an organization, or other human system describes the combination of traditionally administrative personnel functions with acquisition and application of skills, knowledge and experience, Employee Relations and resource planning at various levels. The field draws upon concepts developed in Industrial/Organizational Psychology and System Theory. _____ has at least two related interpretations depending on context. The original usage derives from political economy and economics, where it was traditionally called labor, one of four factors of production although this perspective is changing as a function of new and ongoing research into more strategic approaches at national levels. This first usage is used more in terms of '_____ development', and can go beyond just organizations to the level of nations . The more traditional usage within corporations and businesses refers to the individuals within a firm or agency, and to the portion of the organization that deals with hiring, firing, training, and other personnel issues, typically referred to as `_____ management'.
    a. Progressive discipline
    b. Human resource management
    c. Human resources
    d. Bradford Factor

22. _____ is a term used by inventory specialists to describe a level of extra stock that is maintained below the cycle stock to buffer against stockouts. _____ exists to counter uncertainties in supply and demand. _____ is defined as extra units of inventory carried as protection against possible stockouts .(shortfall in raw material or packaging.)
    a. Process automation
    b. Product life cycle
    c. Safety stock
    d. Knowledge worker

23. _____ is a legally declared inability or impairment of ability of an individual or organization to pay its creditors. Creditors may file a _____ petition against a debtor ('involuntary _____') in an effort to recoup a portion of what they are owed or initiate a restructuring. In the majority of cases, however, _____ is initiated by the debtor (a 'voluntary _____' that is filed by the insolvent individual or organization.)

a. 33 Strategies of War
c. 1990 Clean Air Act
b. Bankruptcy
d. 28-hour day

24. In decision theory and estimation theory, the _____ of an estimator, $\hat{\theta}$, of an unknown parameter of the distribution, θ, is the expected value of the loss function

$$R(\theta, \hat{\theta}) = \mathbb{E}_\theta L(\theta, \hat{\theta}) = \int L(\theta, \hat{\theta})\, dP_\theta.$$

where dP_θ is a probability measure parametrized by θ.

- For a scalar parameter θ and a quadratic loss function,

$$L(\theta, \hat{\theta}) = (\theta - \hat{\theta})^2$$

the _____ function becomes the mean squared error of the estimate,

$$R(\theta, \hat{\theta}) = E_\theta(\theta - \hat{\theta})^2$$

- In density estimation, the unknown parameter is probability density itself. The loss function is typically chosen to be a norm in an appropriate function space. For example, for L^2 norm,

$$L(f, \hat{f}) = \|f - \hat{f}\|_2^2$$

the _____ function becomes the mean integrated squared error

$$R(f, \hat{f}) = E\|f - \hat{f}\|^2$$

a. Financial modeling
c. Risk aversion
b. Linear model
d. Risk

25. _____ is the identification, assessment, and prioritization of risks followed by coordinated and economical application of resources to minimize, monitor, and control the probability and/or impact of unfortunate events.. Risks can come from uncertainty in financial markets, project failures, legal liabilities, credit risk, accidents, natural causes and disasters as well as deliberate attacks from an adversary. Several _____ standards have been developed including the Project Management Institute, the National Institute of Science and Technology, actuarial societies, and ISO standards.
   a. Succession planning
   c. Trademark
   b. Kanban
   d. Risk management

26. _____ is an integrated communications-based process through which individuals and communities discover that existing and newly-identified needs and wants may be satisfied by the products and services of others.

_____ is defined by the American _____ Association as the activity, set of institutions, and processes for creating, communicating, delivering, and exchanging offerings that have value for customers, clients, partners, and society at large. The term developed from the original meaning which referred literally to going to market, as in shopping, or going to a market to buy or sell goods or services.

a. Customer relationship management
b. Market development
c. Disruptive technology
d. Marketing

27. _____ is the incidence or process of transferring ownership of a business, enterprise, agency or public service from the public sector (government) to the private sector (business.) In a broader sense, _____ refers to transfer of any government function to the private sector including governmental functions like revenue collection and law enforcement.

a. Privatization
b. 1990 Clean Air Act
c. Performance reports
d. 28-hour day

28. _____ has been described as the 'process of social influence in which one person can enlist the aid and support of others in the accomplishment of a common task' . A definition more inclusive of followers comes from Alan Keith of Genentech who said '_____ is ultimately about creating a way for people to contribute to making something extraordinary happen.'

_____ is one of the most salient aspects of the organizational context. However, defining _____ has been challenging.

a. Situational leadership
b. Leadership
c. 28-hour day
d. 1990 Clean Air Act

29. An _____ is a survey of public opinion from a particular sample. _____s are usually designed to represent the opinions of a population by conducting a series of questions and then extrapolating generalities in ratio or within confidence intervals.

The first known example of an _____ was a local straw poll conducted by The Harrisburg Pennsylvanian in 1824, showing Andrew Jackson leading John Quincy Adams by 335 votes to 169 in the contest for the United States Presidency.

a. Opinion poll
b. A4e
c. AAAI
d. A Stake in the Outcome

Chapter 3. Legal Implications of Business Arrangements in the Healthcare Industry

1. In economics and sociology, an _____ is any factor (financial or non-financial) that enables or motivates a particular course of action, or counts as a reason for preferring one choice to the alternatives. It is an expectation that encourages people to behave in a certain way. Since human beings are purposeful creatures, the study of _____ structures is central to the study of all economic activity (both in terms of individual decision-making and in terms of co-operation and competition within a larger institutional structure.)
   - a. AAAI
   - b. A Stake in the Outcome
   - c. Incentive
   - d. A4e

2. An _____ is a formal scheme used to promote or encourage specific actions or behavior by a specific group of people during a defined period of time. _____s are particularly used in business management to motivate employees, and in sales in order to attract and retain customers. The scientific literature also refers to this concept as Pay for Performance.
   - a. AAAI
   - b. Incentive program
   - c. A Stake in the Outcome
   - d. A4e

3. _____ is an advertisement in which a particular product specifically mentions a competitor by name for the express purpose of showing why the competitor is inferior to the product naming it.

   This should not be confused with parody advertisements, where a fictional product is being advertised for the purpose of poking fun at the particular advertisement, nor should it be confused with the use of a coined brand name for the purpose of comparing the product without actually naming an actual competitor. ('Wikipedia tastes better and is less filling than the Encyclopedia Galactica.')

   In the 1980s, during what has been referred to as the cola wars, soft-drink manufacturer Pepsi ran a series of advertisements where people, caught on hidden camera, in a blind taste test, chose Pepsi over rival Coca-Cola.
   - a. 28-hour day
   - b. 33 Strategies of War
   - c. 1990 Clean Air Act
   - d. Comparative advertising

4. The _____ is an American federal law which allows people who are not affiliated with the government to file actions against federal contractors claiming fraud against the government. The act of filing such actions is informally called 'whistleblowing.' Persons filing under the Act stand to receive a portion (usually about 15-25 percent) of any recovered damages.
   - a. Personal Responsibility and Work Opportunity Reconciliation Act
   - b. False Claims Act
   - c. Chrapliwy v. Uniroyal
   - d. Bennett Amendment

5. A _____ is an entity formed between two or more parties to undertake economic activity together. The parties agree to create a new entity by both contributing equity, and they then share in the revenues, expenses, and control of the enterprise. The venture can be for one specific project only, or a continuing business relationship such as the Fuji Xerox _____.
   - a. Civil Rights Act of 1991
   - b. Meritor Savings Bank v. Vinson
   - c. Patent
   - d. Joint venture

6. An _____ is a person who has possession of an enterprise and assumes significant accountability for the inherent risks and the outcome. It is an ambitious leader who combines land, labor, and capital to create and market new goods or services. The term is a loanword from French and was first defined by the Irish economist Richard Cantillon.

Chapter 3. Legal Implications of Business Arrangements in the Healthcare Industry

a. AAAI
b. A4e
c. A Stake in the Outcome
d. Entrepreneur

7. _____ generally refers to a list of all planned expenses and revenues. It is a plan for saving and spending. A _____ is an important concept in microeconomics, which uses a _____ line to illustrate the trade-offs between two or more goods.

a. 28-hour day
b. 33 Strategies of War
c. 1990 Clean Air Act
d. Budget

8. _____ is the state or fact of exclusive rights and control over property, which may be an object, land/real estate or intellectual property. An _____ right is also referred to as title. The concept of _____ has existed for thousands of years and in all cultures.

a. A Stake in the Outcome
b. Emanation of the state
c. A4e
d. Ownership

9. _____ is the price at which an asset would trade in a competitive Walrasian auction setting. _____ is often used interchangeably with open _____, fair value or fair _____, although these terms have distinct definitions in different standards, and may differ in some circumstances.

International Valuation Standards defines _____ as 'the estimated amount for which a property should exchange on the date of valuation between a willing buyer and a willing seller in an arm's-length transaction after proper marketing wherein the parties had each acted knowledgeably, prudently, and without compulsion.'

_____ is a concept distinct from market price, which is 'the price at which one can transact', while _____ is 'the true underlying value' according to theoretical standards.

a. Market value added
b. Restructuring
c. Market value
d. Payback period

10. _____ makes a person responsible for the damage and loss caused by his/her acts and omissions regardless of culpability. _____ is important in torts (especially product liability), corporations law, and criminal law.

a. Strict liability
b. Ten year occupational employment projection
c. Competency-based job descriptions
d. Historiometry

11. _____ protects professional practitioners such as architects, home inspectors, lawyers, physicians, and accountants against potential negligence claims made by their patients/clients. _____ may take on different names depending on the profession. For example, _____ in reference to the medical profession may be called Medical Malpractice.

a. Workers compensation
b. 1990 Clean Air Act
c. 28-hour day
d. Professional liability insurance

12. _____ plant, and equipment, is a term used in accountancy for assets and property which cannot easily be converted into cash. This can be compared with current assets such as cash or bank accounts, which are described as liquid assets. In most cases, only tangible assets are referred to as fixed.

a. 33 Strategies of War
c. 28-hour day

b. 1990 Clean Air Act
d. Fixed asset

13. In decision theory and estimation theory, the _____ of an estimator, $\hat{\theta}$, of an unknown parameter of the distribution, θ, is the expected value of the loss function

$$R(\theta, \hat{\theta}) = \mathbb{E}_\theta L(\theta, \hat{\theta}) = \int L(\theta, \hat{\theta})\, dP_\theta.$$

where dP_θ is a probability measure parametrized by θ.

- For a scalar parameter θ and a quadratic loss function,

$$L(\theta, \hat{\theta}) = (\theta - \hat{\theta})^2$$

the _____ function becomes the mean squared error of the estimate,

$$R(\theta, \hat{\theta}) = E_\theta(\theta - \hat{\theta})^2$$

- In density estimation, the unknown parameter is probability density itself. The loss function is typically chosen to be a norm in an appropriate function space. For example, for L^2 norm,

$$L(f, \hat{f}) = \|f - \hat{f}\|_2^2$$

the _____ function becomes the mean integrated squared error

$$R(f, \hat{f}) = E\|f - \hat{f}\|^2$$

a. Risk aversion
c. Linear model

b. Financial modeling
d. Risk

Chapter 3. Legal Implications of Business Arrangements in the Healthcare Industry

14. _____, known in the United States as antitrust law, has three main elements:

- prohibiting agreements or practices that restrict free trading and competition between business entities. This includes in particular the repression of cartels.
- banning abusive behavior by a firm dominating a market, or anti-competitive practices that tend to lead to such a dominant position. Practices controlled in this way may include predatory pricing, tying, price gouging, refusal to deal, and many others.
- supervising the mergers and acquisitions of large corporations, including some joint ventures. Transactions that are considered to threaten the competitive process can be prohibited altogether, or approved subject to 'remedies' such as an obligation to divest part of the merged business or to offer licenses or access to facilities to enable other businesses to continue competing.

The substance and practice of _____ varies from jurisdiction to jurisdiction. Protecting the interests of consumers (consumer welfare) and ensuring that entrepreneurs have an opportunity to compete in the market economy are often treated as important objectives. _____ is closely connected with law on deregulation of access to markets, state aids and subsidies, the privatization of state owned assets and the establishment of independent sector regulators. In recent decades, _____ has been viewed as a way to provide better public services.

- a. Rulemaking
- b. Right to Financial Privacy Act
- c. Competition law
- d. Federal Employers Liability Act

15. In microeconomics and strategic management, the term _____ describes a type of ownership and control. It is a strategy used by a business or corporation that seeks to sell a type of product in numerous markets. _____ in marketing is much more common than vertical integration is in production.

- a. Farmshoring
- b. Career development
- c. No-bid contract
- d. Horizontal integration

16. A _____ is a compensation, usually financial, received by a worker in exchange for their labor.

Compensation in terms of _____s is given to worker and compensation in terms of salary is given to employees. Compensation is a monetary benefits given to employees in returns of the services provided by them.

- a. State Compensation Insurance Fund
- b. Profit-sharing agreement
- c. Wage
- d. Performance-related pay

17. The _____ is an independent agency of the United States government, established in 1914 by the _____ Act. Its principal mission is the promotion of 'consumer protection' and the elimination and prevention of what regulators perceive to be harmfully 'anti-competitive' business practices, such as coercive monopoly.

The _____ Act was one of President Wilson's major acts against trusts.

- a. Federal Trade Commission
- b. 33 Strategies of War
- c. 28-hour day
- d. 1990 Clean Air Act

18. The _____ is a set of amendments to the antitrust laws of the United States, principally the Clayton Antitrust Act. The HSR Act was signed into law by President Gerald R. Ford on September 30, 1976. The context in which the HSR Act is usually cited is 15 U.S.C.

a. 33 Strategies of War

b. 28-hour day

c. 1990 Clean Air Act

d. Hart-Scott-Rodino Antitrust Improvements Act of 1976

Chapter 4. Stakeholder Management—Strategies and Styles

1. _____ comprises the actual output or results of an organization as measured against its intended outputs (or goals and objectives.)

Specialists in many fields are concerned with _____ including strategic planners, operations, finance, legal, and organizational development.

In recent years, many organizations have attempted to manage _____ using the balanced scorecard methodology where performance is tracked and measured in multiple dimensions such as:

- financial performance (e.g. shareholder return)
- customer service
- social responsibility (e.g. corporate citizenship, community outreach)
- employee stewardship

a. A4e
b. Organizational performance
c. A Stake in the Outcome
d. AAAI

2. Various _____ can be employed dependent on the culture of the business, the nature of the task, the nature of the workforce and the personality and skills of the leaders. This idea was further developed by Robert Tannenbaum and Warren H. Schmidt (1958, 1973) who argued that the style of leadership is dependent upon the prevailing circumstance; therefore leaders should exercise a range of leadership styles and should deploy them as appropriate.

An Autocratic or authoritarian manager makes all the decisions, keeping the information and decision making among the senior management.

a. 33 Strategies of War
b. 1990 Clean Air Act
c. 28-hour day
d. Management styles

3. In finance and economics, _____ or divestiture is the reduction of some kind of asset for either financial or ethical objectives or sale of an existing business by a firm. A _____ is the opposite of an investment.

a. 1990 Clean Air Act
b. 28-hour day
c. 33 Strategies of War
d. Divestment

4. A _____ is a formal relationship between two or more parties to pursue a set of agreed upon goals or to meet a critical business need while remaining independent organizations.

Partners may provide the _____ with resources such as products, distribution channels, manufacturing capability, project funding, capital equipment, knowledge, expertise, or intellectual property. The alliance is a cooperation or collaboration which aims for a synergy where each partner hopes that the benefits from the alliance will be greater than those from individual efforts.

a. Process automation
b. Farmshoring
c. Golden parachute
d. Strategic alliance

Chapter 4. Stakeholder Management—Strategies and Styles

5. A _____ is an alliance among individuals or groups, during which they cooperate in joint action, each in his own self-interest, joining forces together for a common cause. This alliance may be temporary or a matter of convenience. A _____ thus differs from a more formal covenant.
   a. 28-hour day
   b. Coalition
   c. 33 Strategies of War
   d. 1990 Clean Air Act

6. _____ is one of the managerial functions like planning, organizing, staffing and directing. It is an important function because it helps to check the errors and to take the corrective action so that deviation from standards are minimized and stated goals of the organization are achieved in desired manner. According to modern concepts, _____ is a foreseeing action whereas earlier concept of _____ was used only when errors were detected. _____ in management means setting standards, measuring actual performance and taking corrective action.
   a. Turnover
   b. Decision tree pruning
   c. Schedule of reinforcement
   d. Control

7. _____ is an advertisement in which a particular product specifically mentions a competitor by name for the express purpose of showing why the competitor is inferior to the product naming it.

This should not be confused with parody advertisements, where a fictional product is being advertised for the purpose of poking fun at the particular advertisement, nor should it be confused with the use of a coined brand name for the purpose of comparing the product without actually naming an actual competitor. ('Wikipedia tastes better and is less filling than the Encyclopedia Galactica.')

In the 1980s, during what has been referred to as the cola wars, soft-drink manufacturer Pepsi ran a series of advertisements where people, caught on hidden camera, in a blind taste test, chose Pepsi over rival Coca-Cola.

   a. 28-hour day
   b. Comparative advertising
   c. 33 Strategies of War
   d. 1990 Clean Air Act

8. _____ is a recursive process where two or more people or organizations work together in an intersection of common goals -- for example, an intellectual endeavor that is creative in nature--by sharing knowledge, learning and building consensus. _____ does not require leadership and can sometimes bring better results through decentralization and egalitarianism. In particular, teams that work collaboratively can obtain greater resources, recognition and reward when facing competition for finite resources. _____ is also present in opposing goals exhibiting the notion of adversarial _____, though this is not a common case for using the term.
   a. 1990 Clean Air Act
   b. Collaboration
   c. Collectivism
   d. 28-hour day

Chapter 4. Stakeholder Management—Strategies and Styles

9. _____ is an increasingly broadening term with which an organization, or other human system describes the combination of traditionally administrative personnel functions with acquisition and application of skills, knowledge and experience, Employee Relations and resource planning at various levels. The field draws upon concepts developed in Industrial/Organizational Psychology and System Theory. _____ has at least two related interpretations depending on context. The original usage derives from political economy and economics, where it was traditionally called labor, one of four factors of production although this perspective is changing as a function of new and ongoing research into more strategic approaches at national levels. This first usage is used more in terms of '_____ development', and can go beyond just organizations to the level of nations . The more traditional usage within corporations and businesses refers to the individuals within a firm or agency, and to the portion of the organization that deals with hiring, firing, training, and other personnel issues, typically referred to as `_____ management'.
   a. Progressive discipline
   b. Human resources
   c. Human resource management
   d. Bradford Factor

10. _____ is the incidence or process of transferring ownership of a business, enterprise, agency or public service from the public sector (government) to the private sector (business.) In a broader sense, _____ refers to transfer of any government function to the private sector including governmental functions like revenue collection and law enforcement.
   a. 28-hour day
   b. 1990 Clean Air Act
   c. Performance reports
   d. Privatization

11. In game theory, an _____ is a set of moves or strategies taken by the players, or their payoffs resulting from the actions or strategies taken by all players. The two are complementary in that given knowledge of the set of strategies of all players, the final state of the game is known, as are any relevant payoffs. In a game where chance or a random event is involved, the _____ is not known from only the set of strategies, but is only realized when the random event(s) are realized.
   a. Outcome
   b. A Stake in the Outcome
   c. AAAI
   d. A4e

12. _____ refers to the aggregated strategies of single business firm or a strategic business unit (SBU) in a diversified corporation. According to Michael Porter, a firm must formulate a _____ that incorporates either cost leadership, differentiation or focus in order to achieve a sustainable competitive advantage and long-term success in its chosen arenas or industries.

Functional strategies include marketing strategies, new product development strategies, human resource strategies, financial strategies, legal strategies, supply-chain strategies, and information technology management strategies.

   a. Competitive heterogeneity
   b. Strategic thinking
   c. Switching cost
   d. Business strategy

13. The _____ of a company or public agency is the corporate officer primarily responsible for managing the financial risks of the business or agency. This officer is also responsible for financial planning and record-keeping, as well as financial reporting to higher management. (In recent years, however, the role has expanded to encompass communicating financial performance and forecasts to the analyst community.)
   a. 28-hour day
   b. Chief financial officer
   c. 33 Strategies of War
   d. 1990 Clean Air Act

Chapter 4. Stakeholder Management—Strategies and Styles

14. _____ is an integrated communications-based process through which individuals and communities discover that existing and newly-identified needs and wants may be satisfied by the products and services of others.

_____ is defined by the American _____ Association as the activity, set of institutions, and processes for creating, communicating, delivering, and exchanging offerings that have value for customers, clients, partners, and society at large. The term developed from the original meaning which referred literally to going to market, as in shopping, or going to a market to buy or sell goods or services.

- a. Market development
- b. Marketing
- c. Customer relationship management
- d. Disruptive technology

15. _____ is the process in which ideas and objects are recognized, differentiated and understood. _____ implies that objects are grouped into categories, usually for some specific purpose. Ideally, a category illuminates a relationship between the subjects and objects of knowledge.
- a. 1990 Clean Air Act
- b. 33 Strategies of War
- c. 28-hour day
- d. Categorization

Chapter 5. Financial Management of Organized Health Care Delivery Systems

1. _____ is the term used to refer to the standard framework of guidelines for financial accounting used in any given jurisdiction. _____ includes the standards, conventions, and rules accountants follow in recording and summarizing transactions, and in the preparation of financial statements.

Financial accounting is information that must be assembled and reported objectively.

- a. Net income
- c. Treasury stock
- b. Depreciation
- d. Generally accepted accounting principles

2. _____ are formal records of the financial activities of a business, person, or other entity. In British English, including United Kingdom company law, _____ are often referred to as accounts, although the term _____ is also used, particularly by accountants.

_____ provide an overview of a business or person's financial condition in both short and long term.

- a. 28-hour day
- c. Financial statements
- b. 33 Strategies of War
- d. 1990 Clean Air Act

3. _____ refers to the movement of cash into or out of a business or financial product. It is usually measured during a specified, finite period of time. Measurement of _____ can be used

- to determine a project's rate of return or value. The time of _____s into and out of projects are used as inputs in financial models such as internal rate of return, and net present value.
- to determine problems with a business's liquidity. Being profitable does not necessarily mean being liquid. A company can fail because of a shortage of cash, even while profitable.
- as an alternate measure of a business's profits when it is believed that accrual accounting concepts do not represent economic realities. For example, a company may be notionally profitable but generating little operational cash (as may be the case for a company that barters its products rather than selling for cash.) In such a case, the company may be deriving additional operating cash by issuing shares evaluating default risk, re-investment requirements, etc.

_____ is a generic term used differently depending on the context. It may be defined by users for their own purposes.

- a. Gross profit margin
- c. Gross profit
- b. Sweat equity
- d. Cash flow

4. In business and accounting, _____s are everything of value that is owned by a person or company. Any property or object of value that one possesses, usually considered as applicable to the payment of one's debts is considered an _____. Simplistically stated, _____s are things of value that can be readily converted into cash.

- a. Asset
- c. AAAI
- b. A Stake in the Outcome
- d. A4e

5. In accounting, a _____ is an asset on the balance sheet which is expected to be sold or otherwise used up in the near future, usually within one year, or one business cycle - whichever is longer. Typical _____s include cash, cash equivalents, accounts receivable, inventory, the portion of prepaid accounts which will be used within a year, and short-term investments.

Chapter 5. Financial Management of Organized Health Care Delivery Systems 21

On the balance sheet, assets will typically be classified into _____s and long-term assets.

a. Net income
c. Treasury stock
b. Current asset
d. Matching principle

6. _____ plant, and equipment, is a term used in accountancy for assets and property which cannot easily be converted into cash. This can be compared with current assets such as cash or bank accounts, which are described as liquid assets. In most cases, only tangible assets are referred to as fixed.

a. 28-hour day
c. 1990 Clean Air Act
b. 33 Strategies of War
d. Fixed asset

7. The phrase mergers and _____s refers to the aspect of corporate strategy, corporate finance and management dealing with the buying, selling and combining of different companies that can aid, finance, or help a growing company in a given industry grow rapidly without having to create another business entity.

An _____, also known as a takeover or a buyout, is the buying of one company (the 'target') by another. An _____ may be friendly or hostile.

a. Acquisition
c. AAAI
b. A Stake in the Outcome
d. A4e

8. In finance, _____ are considered liabilities of the business that are to be settled in cash within the fiscal year or the operating cycle, whichever period is longer.

For example accounts payable for goods, services or supplies that were purchased for use in the operation of the business and payable within a normal period of time would be _____.

Bonds, mortgages and loans that are payable over a term exceeding one year would be fixed liabilities.

a. Current liabilities
c. Matching principle
b. Generally accepted accounting principles
d. Depreciation

9. In general, a _____ is an arrangement to provide people with an income when they are no longer earning a regular income from employment.

The terms retirement plan or superannuation refer to a _____ granted upon retirement . Retirement plans may be set up by employers, insurance companies, the government or other institutions such as employer associations or trade unions.

a. Pension insurance contract
c. State Compensation Insurance Fund
b. Wage
d. Pension

Chapter 5. Financial Management of Organized Health Care Delivery Systems

10. The _____ of an edge is $c_f(u, v) = c(u, v) - f(u, v)$. This defines a residual network denoted $G_f(V, E_f)$, giving the amount of available capacity. See that there can be an edge from u to v in the residual network, even though there is no edge from u to v in the original network.

   a. Residual capacity
   b. 33 Strategies of War
   c. 1990 Clean Air Act
   d. 28-hour day

11. In economics, business, retail, and accounting, a _____ is the value of money that has been used up to produce something, and hence is not available for use anymore. In economics, a _____ is an alternative that is given up as a result of a decision. In business, the _____ may be one of acquisition, in which case the amount of money expended to acquire it is counted as _____.

   a. Cost
   b. Cost allocation
   c. Cost overrun
   d. Fixed costs

12. An _____ is the annual budget of an activity stated in terms of Budget Classification Code, functional/subfunctional categories and cost accounts. It contains estimates of the total value of resources required for the performance of the operation including reimbursable work or services for others. It also includes estimates of workload in terms of total work units identified by cost accounts.

   a. Operating budget
   b. Expected return
   c. Inflation rate
   d. Expected gain

13. _____ generally refers to a list of all planned expenses and revenues. It is a plan for saving and spending. A _____ is an important concept in microeconomics, which uses a _____ line to illustrate the trade-offs between two or more goods.

   a. 1990 Clean Air Act
   b. 28-hour day
   c. 33 Strategies of War
   d. Budget

14. In finance, a _____ or accounting ratio is a ratio of two selected numerical values taken from an enterprise's financial statements. There are many standard ratios used to try to evaluate the overall financial condition of a corporation or other organization. _____s may be used by managers within a firm, by current and potential shareholders (owners) of a firm, and by a firm's creditors.

   a. Rate of return
   b. Financial ratio
   c. Return on equity
   d. Return on sales

15. _____, net margin, net _____ or net profit ratio all refer to a measure of profitability. It is calculated by finding the net profit as a percentage of the revenue.

$$\text{Net profit margin} = \frac{\text{Net profit (after taxes)}}{\text{Revenue}} \times 100\%$$

The _____ is mostly used for internal comparison.

   a. Profit maximization
   b. Net profit margin
   c. Profit margin
   d. 1990 Clean Air Act

16. The _____ percentage shows how profitable a company's assets are in generating revenue.

Chapter 5. Financial Management of Organized Health Care Delivery Systems 23

_____ can be computed as:

$$ROA = \frac{\text{Net Income} + \text{Interest Expense} - \text{Interest Tax savings}}{\text{Average Total Assets}}$$

This number tells you what the company can do with what it has, i.e. how many dollars of earnings they derive from each dollar of assets they control. Its a useful number for comparing competing companies in the same industry.

a. Return on Capital Employed
c. P/E ratio
b. Return on equity
d. Return on assets

17. _____(requity)measures the rate of return on the ownership interest (shareholders' equity) of the common stock owners. It measures a firm's efficiency at generating profits from every dollar of shareholders' equity (also known as net assets or assets minus liabilities.) It shows how well a company uses investment dollars to generate earnings growth.

a. Rate of return
c. Return on Capital Employed
b. Financial ratio
d. Return on equity

18. The _____ is a financial ratio that measures whether or not a firm has enough resources to pay its debts over the next 12 months. It compares a firm's current assets to its current liabilities. It is expressed as follows:

$$\text{Current ratio} = \frac{\text{Current Assets}}{\text{Current Liabilities}}$$

For example, if WXY Company's current assets are $50,000,000 and its current liabilities are $40,000,000, then its _____ would be $50,000,000 divided by $40,000,000, which equals 1.25.

a. Times interest earned
c. Financial ratio
b. Current ratio
d. Return on assets

19. In financial accounting, _____ , cash flow provided by operations or cash flow from operating activities, refers to the amount of cash a company generates from the revenues it brings in, excluding costs associated with long-term investment on capital items or investment in securities.

_____ = Cash generated from operations less taxation and interest paid, investment income received and less dividends paid gives rise to _____s per International Financial Reporting Standards.

To calculate cash generated from operations, one must calculate cash generated from customers and cash paid to suppliers.

a. AAAI
c. A Stake in the Outcome
b. A4e
d. Operating cash flow

Chapter 5. Financial Management of Organized Health Care Delivery Systems

20. Market _____ is a business, economics or investment term that refers to an asset's ability to be easily converted through an act of buying or selling without causing a significant movement in the price and with minimum loss of value. Money, or cash on hand, is the most liquid asset. An act of exchange of a less liquid asset with a more liquid asset is called liquidation.
   a. 28-hour day
   b. 33 Strategies of War
   c. 1990 Clean Air Act
   d. Liquidity

21. In decision theory and estimation theory, the _____ of an estimator, $\hat{\theta}$, of an unknown parameter of the distribution, θ, is the expected value of the loss function

$$R(\theta, \hat{\theta}) = \mathbb{E}_\theta L(\theta, \hat{\theta}) = \int L(\theta, \hat{\theta})\, dP_\theta.$$

where dP_θ is a probability measure parametrized by θ.

- For a scalar parameter θ and a quadratic loss function,

$$L(\theta, \hat{\theta}) = (\theta - \hat{\theta})^2$$

the _____ function becomes the mean squared error of the estimate,

$$R(\theta, \hat{\theta}) = E_\theta (\theta - \hat{\theta})^2$$

- In density estimation, the unknown parameter is probability density itself. The loss function is typically chosen to be a norm in an appropriate function space. For example, for L^2 norm,

$$L(f, \hat{f}) = \|f - \hat{f}\|_2^2$$

the _____ function becomes the mean integrated squared error

$$R(f, \hat{f}) = E\|f - \hat{f}\|^2$$

   a. Financial modeling
   b. Risk
   c. Linear model
   d. Risk aversion

22. In finance, _____ is borrowing money to supplement existing funds for investment in such a way that the potential positive or negative outcome is magnified and/or enhanced. It generally refers to using borrowed funds, or debt, so as to attempt to increase the returns to equity. Deleveraging is the action of reducing borrowings.
   a. Limited partners
   b. Private equity
   c. Limited liability corporation
   d. Gearing

Chapter 5. Financial Management of Organized Health Care Delivery Systems

23. In economics and government finance, _____ is the ratio of debt service payments of a country to that country's export earnings. A country's international finances are healthier when this ratio is low. The ratio is between 0 and 20% for most countries.
    a. 28-hour day
    b. 1990 Clean Air Act
    c. 33 Strategies of War
    d. Debt service ratio

24. _____ is an advertisement in which a particular product specifically mentions a competitor by name for the express purpose of showing why the competitor is inferior to the product naming it.

    This should not be confused with parody advertisements, where a fictional product is being advertised for the purpose of poking fun at the particular advertisement, nor should it be confused with the use of a coined brand name for the purpose of comparing the product without actually naming an actual competitor. ('Wikipedia tastes better and is less filling than the Encyclopedia Galactica.')

    In the 1980s, during what has been referred to as the cola wars, soft-drink manufacturer Pepsi ran a series of advertisements where people, caught on hidden camera, in a blind taste test, chose Pepsi over rival Coca-Cola.

    a. 28-hour day
    b. 1990 Clean Air Act
    c. Comparative advertising
    d. 33 Strategies of War

25. The _____ is a performance management tool for measuring whether the smaller-scale operational activities of a company are aligned with its larger-scale objectives in terms of vision and strategy.

    By focusing not only on financial outcomes but also on the operational, marketing and developmental inputs to these, the _____ helps provide a more comprehensive view of a business, which in turn helps organizations act in their best long-term interests. This tool is also being used to address business response to climate change and greenhouse gas emissions.

    a. Commercial management
    b. Middle management
    c. Management development
    d. Balanced scorecard

26. _____ is the process of comparing the cost, cycle time, productivity, or quality of a specific process or method to another that is widely considered to be an industry standard or best practice. Essentially, _____ provides a snapshot of the performance of your business and helps you understand where you are in relation to a particular standard. The result is often a business case for making changes in order to make improvements.
    a. Complementors
    b. Competitive heterogeneity
    c. Cost leadership
    d. Benchmarking

27. A _____ is the belief that there is a technique, method, process, activity, incentive or reward that is more effective at delivering a particular outcome than any other technique, method, process, etc. The idea is that with proper processes, checks, and testing, a desired outcome can be delivered with fewer problems and unforeseen complications. _____s can also be defined as the most efficient (least amount of effort) and effective (best results) way of accomplishing a task, based on repeatable procedures that have proven themselves over time for large numbers of people.
    a. Design management
    b. Fix it twice
    c. Hierarchical organization
    d. Best practice

Chapter 5. Financial Management of Organized Health Care Delivery Systems

28. _____ refers to an assessment of the viability, stability and profitability of a business, sub-business or project.

It is performed by professionals who prepare reports using ratios that make use of information taken from financial statements and other reports. These reports are usually presented to top management as one of their bases in making business decisions.

  a. Financial analysis
  b. 28-hour day
  c. 33 Strategies of War
  d. 1990 Clean Air Act

29. In financial accounting, a _____ or statement of financial position is a summary of a person's or organization's balances. Assets, liabilities and ownership equity are listed as of a specific date, such as the end of its financial year. A _____ is often described as a snapshot of a company's financial condition.
  a. 1990 Clean Air Act
  b. 33 Strategies of War
  c. 28-hour day
  d. Balance sheet

30. _____ can be regarded as an outcome of mental processes (cognitive process) leading to the selection of a course of action among several alternatives. Every _____ process produces a final choice. The output can be an action or an opinion of choice.
  a. 28-hour day
  b. 33 Strategies of War
  c. Decision making
  d. 1990 Clean Air Act

31. _____ is the value on a given date of a future payment or series of future payments, discounted to reflect the time value of money and other factors such as investment risk. _____ calculations are widely used in business and economics to provide a means to compare cash flows at different times on a meaningful 'like to like' basis.

If offered a choice between $100 today or $100 in one year, everyone will choose $100 today.

  a. 1990 Clean Air Act
  b. Net present value
  c. Discounted cash flow
  d. Present value

32. Simply put, _____ is the value of money figuring in a given amount of interest for a given amount of time. For example 100 dollars of today's money held for a year at 5 percent interest is worth 105 dollars, therefore 100 dollars paid now or 105 dollars paid exactly one year from now is the same amount of payment of money with that given interest at that given amount of time. This notion dates at least to Martín de Azpilcueta of the School of Salamanca.
  a. Financial modeling
  b. Panjer recursion
  c. Risk aversion
  d. Time value of money

33. The _____ is a rate of return used in capital budgeting to measure and compare the profitability of investments. It is also called the discounted cash flow rate of return (DCFROR) or simply the rate of return (ROR.) In the context of savings and loans the IRR is also called the effective interest rate.
  a. A Stake in the Outcome
  b. A4e
  c. AAAI
  d. Internal rate of return

34. _____ or net present worth (NPW) is defined as the total present value (PV) of a time series of cash flows. It is a standard method for using the time value of money to appraise long-term projects. Used for capital budgeting, and widely throughout economics, it measures the excess or shortfall of cash flows, in present value terms, once financing charges are met.

a. Present value
b. Discounted cash flow
c. 1990 Clean Air Act
d. Net present value

35. _____ identifies the relationship of investment to payoff of a proposed project. The ratio is calculated as follows:

$$\text{Profitability index} = \frac{\text{PV of future cash flows}}{\text{PV of initial investment}}$$

_____ is also known as Profit Investment Ratio, abbreviated to P.I. and Value Investment Ratio (V.I.R.). _____ is a good tool for ranking projects because it allows you to clearly identify the amount of value created per unit of investment, thus if you are capital constrained you wish to invest in those projects which create value most efficiently first.

Nota Bene; Statements below this paragraph assume the cash flow calculated does not include the investment made in the project.

a. Profitability index
b. 1990 Clean Air Act
c. 28-hour day
d. Demand forecasting

36. In finance, _____, is the ratio of money gained or lost on an investment relative to the amount of money invested. The amount of money gained or lost may be referred to as interest, profit/loss, gain/loss, or net income/loss. The money invested may be referred to as the asset, capital, principal, or the cost basis of the investment.

a. Return on sales
b. Financial ratio
c. Return on Capital Employed
d. Rate of return

37. _____ is a term used in accounting, economics and finance to spread the cost of an asset over the span of several years.

In simple words we can say that _____ is the reduction in the value of an asset due to usage, passage of time, wear and tear, technological outdating or obsolescence, depletion, inadequacy, rot, rust, decay or other such factors.

In accounting, _____ is a term used to describe any method of attributing the historical or purchase cost of an asset across its useful life, roughly corresponding to normal wear and tear.

a. Matching principle
b. Net profit
c. Depreciation
d. Treasury stock

38. The _____ is an interest rate a central bank charges depository institutions that borrow reserves from it.

Chapter 5. Financial Management of Organized Health Care Delivery Systems

The term _____ has two meanings:

- the same as interest rate; the term 'discount' does not refer to the meaning of the word, but to the purpose of using the quantity, such as computations of present value, e.g. net present value or discounted cash flow

- the annual effective _____, which is the annual interest divided by the capital including that interest; this rate is lower than the interest rate; it corresponds to using the value after a year as the nominal value, and seeing the initial value as the nominal value minus a discount; it is used for Treasury Bills and similar financial instruments

The annual effective _____ is the annual interest divided by the capital including that interest, which is the interest rate divided by 100% plus the interest rate. It is the annual discount factor to be applied to the future cash flow, to find the discount, subtracted from a future value to find the value one year earlier.

For example, suppose there is a government bond that sells for $95 and pays $100 in a year's time.

a. 28-hour day
b. 1990 Clean Air Act
c. 33 Strategies of War
d. Discount rate

39. _____ in business and economics refers to the period of time required for the return on an investment to 'repay' the sum of the original investment. For example, a $1000 investment which returned $500 per year would have a two year _____. It intuitively measures how long something takes to 'pay for itself.' Shorter _____s are obviously preferable to longer _____s (all else being equal.)

a. Novated lease
b. Net worth
c. Market value
d. Payback period

40. The term _____ usually refers to a weighted arithmetic mean, but weighted versions of other means can also be calculated, such as the weighted geometric mean and the weighted harmonic mean.

Given two school classes, one with 20 students, and one with 30 students, the grades in each class on a test were:

Morning class = 62, 67, 71, 74, 76, 77, 78, 79, 79, 80, 80, 81, 81, 82, 83, 84, 86, 89, 93, 98

Afternoon class = 81, 82, 83, 84, 85, 86, 87, 87, 88, 88, 89, 89, 89, 90, 90, 90, 90, 91, 91, 91, 92, 92, 93, 93, 94, 95, 96, 97, 98, 99

The straight average for the morning class is 80 and the straight average of the afternoon class is 90. The straight average of 80 and 90 is 85, the mean of the two class means.

a. 1990 Clean Air Act
b. 28-hour day
c. Weighted average
d. 33 Strategies of War

Chapter 5. Financial Management of Organized Health Care Delivery Systems

41. The _____ is the rate (expressed as a percentage, like interest) that a company is expected to pay to debtholders (cost of debt) and shareholders (cost of equity) to finance its assets.

WACC is the minimum return that a company must earn on existing asset base to satisfy its creditors, owners, and other providers of capital. Companies raise money from a number of sources: common equity, preferred equity, straight debt, convertible debt, exchangeable debt, warrants, options, pension liabilities, executive stock options, governmental subsidies, and so on.

a. 1990 Clean Air Act
b. Cost of capital
c. Capital intensive
d. Weighted average cost of capital

42. The _____ is an expected return that the provider of capital plans to earn on their investment.

Capital (money) used for funding a business should earn returns for the capital providers who risk their capital. For an investment to be worthwhile, the expected return on capital must be greater than the _____.

a. Capital intensive
b. 1990 Clean Air Act
c. Weighted average cost of capital
d. Cost of capital

43. In finance, _____ refers to the way a corporation finances its assets through some combination of equity, debt, or hybrid securities. A firm's _____ is then the composition or 'structure' of its liabilities. For example, a firm that sells $20 billion in equity and $80 billion in debt is said to be 20% equity-financed and 80% debt-financed.

a. Shareholder value
b. Gross profit margin
c. Capital budgeting
d. Capital structure

44. _____ is the capital that a business raises by taking out a loan. It is a loan made to a company that is normally repaid at some future date. _____ differs from equity or share capital because subscribers to _____ do not become part owners of the business, but are merely creditors, and the suppliers of _____ usually receive a contractually fixed annual percentage return on their loan, and this is known as the coupon rate.

a. Net worth
b. Novated lease
c. Market value added
d. Debt capital

45. An _____ is a practitioner of accountancy, which is the measurement, disclosure or provision of assurance about financial information that helps managers, investors, tax authorities and other decision makers make resource allocation decisions.

The word '_____' is derived from the French 'Compter' which took its origin from the Latin 'Computare'. The word was formerly written in English as 'Accomptant', but in process of time the word, which was always pronounced by dropping the 'p', became gradually changed both in pronunciation and in orthography to its present form.

a. A4e
b. A Stake in the Outcome
c. AAAI
d. Accountant

Chapter 5. Financial Management of Organized Health Care Delivery Systems

46. _____ is an organization's process of defining its strategy and making decisions on allocating its resources to pursue this strategy, including its capital and people. Various business analysis techniques can be used in _____, including SWOT analysis (Strengths, Weaknesses, Opportunities, and Threats) and PEST analysis (Political, Economic, Social, and Technological analysis) or STEER analysis involving Socio-cultural, Technological, Economic, Ecological, and Regulatory factors and EPISTEL (Environment, Political, Informatic, Social, Technological, Economic and Legal)

_____ is the formal consideration of an organization's future course. All _____ deals with at least one of three key questions:

1. 'What do we do?'
2. 'For whom do we do it?'
3. 'How do we excel?'

In business _____, the third question is better phrased 'How can we beat or avoid competition?'. (Bradford and Duncan, page 1.)

a. 33 Strategies of War
b. 1990 Clean Air Act
c. 28-hour day
d. Strategic planning

47. _____ refers to metrics and measures of output from production processes, per unit of input. Labor _____, for example, is typically measured as a ratio of output per labor-hour, an input. _____ may be conceived of as a metrics of the technical or engineering efficiency of production.

a. Master production schedule
b. Value engineering
c. Remanufacturing
d. Productivity

48. The maturity road mapping method (MRMM) is a general procedure to increase the speed and reduce the cost of achieving the maturity condition in a process, product or an organization and with similar approach like PDCA and we call it as _____.

This methodology was developed from 1985 and completed during more than two decades. The basic elements of this model are three as follows; 1- software 2- hardware 3- roadware

Book over of MRM Components of economic growth through productivity (Saari 2006)

The logical manner of this approach is like the periodic table of the chemical elements(by Dmitri Mendeleev) that with defining the trend of electron circulation around cell of the atom helps understanding and predicting unknown atoms.

a. Gross domestic product
b. Productivity management
c. Deflation
d. Perfect competition

49. In economics, _____ are business expenses that are not dependent on the activities of the business They tend to be time-related, such as salaries or rents being paid per month. This is in contrast to variable costs, which are volume-related (and are paid per quantity.)

Chapter 5. Financial Management of Organized Health Care Delivery Systems   31

In management accounting, _____ are defined as expenses that do not change in proportion to the activity of a business, within the relevant period or scale of production.

a. Cost of quality
c. Cost allocation
b. Fixed costs
d. Transaction cost

50. _____s are expenses that change in proportion to the activity of a business. In other words, _____ is the sum of marginal costs. It can also be considered normal costs.

a. Variable cost
c. Fixed costs
b. Cost accounting
d. Cost overrun

51. In economics ' business, specifically cost accounting, the _____ is the point at which cost or expenses and revenue are equal: there is no net loss or gain, and one has 'broken even'. A profit or a loss has not been made, although opportunity costs have been paid, and capital has received the risk-adjusted, expected return.

For example, if the business sells less than 200 tables each month, it will make a loss, if it sells more, it will be a profit.

a. Fixed asset turnover
c. Defined benefit pension plan
b. Break-even point
d. Virtuous circle

52. In cost-volume-profit analysis, a form of management accounting, _____ is the marginal profit per unit sale. It is a useful quantity in carrying out various calculations, and can be used as a measure of operating leverage.

The Total _____ is Total Revenue (TR, or Sales) minus Total Variable Cost (TVC):

TContribution margin = TR − TVC

The Unit _____ (C) is Unit Revenue (Price, P) minus Unit Variable Cost (V):

C = P − V

The _____ Ratio is the percentage of Contribution over Total Revenue, which can be calculated from the unit contribution over unit price or total contribution over Total Revenue:

$$\frac{C}{P} = \frac{P-V}{P} = \frac{\text{Unit Contribution Margin}}{\text{Price}} = \frac{\text{Total Contribution Margin}}{\text{Total Revenue}}$$

For instance, if the price is $10 and the unit variable cost is $2, then the unit _____ is $8, and the _____ ratio is $8/$10 = 80%.

a. Profit center
c. Customer profitability
b. Factory overhead
d. Contribution margin

Chapter 5. Financial Management of Organized Health Care Delivery Systems

53. _____ is a costing model that identifies activities in an organization and assigns the cost of each activity resource to all products and services according to the actual consumption by each: it assigns more indirect costs (overhead) into direct costs.

In this way an organization can establish the true cost of its individual products and services for the purposes of identifying and eliminating those which are unprofitable and lowering the prices of those which are overpriced.

In a business organization, the ABC methodology assigns an organization's resource costs through activities to the products and services provided to its customers.

   a. A4e
   b. Indirect costs
   c. A Stake in the Outcome
   d. Activity-based costing

54. The _____ is a measure of how revenue growth translates into growth in operating income. It is a measure of leverage, and of how risky (volatile) a company's operating income is.

There are various measures of _____, which can be interpreted analogously to financial leverage.

   a. A4e
   b. AAAI
   c. A Stake in the Outcome
   d. Operating leverage

55. _____ is a pricing method used by firms. It is defined as 'a cost management tool for reducing the overall cost of a product over its entire life-cycle with the help of production, engineering, research and design'. A target cost is the maximum amount of cost that can be incurred on a product and with it the firm can still earn the required profit margin from that product at a particular selling price.

   a. Pricing
   b. Price war
   c. Pricing objectives
   d. Target costing

56. _____ is a concept in ethics with several meanings. It is often used synonymously with such concepts as responsibility, answerability, enforcement, blameworthiness, liability and other terms associated with the expectation of account-giving. As an aspect of governance, it has been central to discussions related to problems in both the public and private (corporation) worlds.

   a. Usury
   b. A4e
   c. A Stake in the Outcome
   d. Accountability

57. _____ or contract administration is the management of contracts made with customers, vendors, partners, or employees. _____ includes negotiating the terms and conditions in contracts and ensuring compliance with the terms and conditions, as well as documenting and agreeing any changes that may arise during its implementation or execution. It can be summarized as the process of systematically and efficiently managing contract creating, execution, and analysis for the purpose of maximizing financial and operational performance and minimizing risk.

   a. World Trade Organization
   b. 1990 Clean Air Act
   c. Contract management
   d. Network planning and design

58. In finance, the _____ approach describes a method of valuing a project, company, or asset using the concepts of the time value of money. All future cash flows are estimated and discounted to give their present values. The discount rate used is generally the appropriate WACC, that reflects the risk of the cashflows.

a. Discounted cash flow
b. Net present value
c. 1990 Clean Air Act
d. Present value

Chapter 6. Human Resources Management in Organized Delivery Systems

1. _____ is a system of training a new generation of practitioners of a skill. Apprentices (or in early modern usage 'prentices') or prot>ég>és build their careers from _____s. Most of their training is done on the job while working for an employer who helps the apprentices learn their trade, in exchange for their continuing labour for an agreed period after they become skilled.
   a. AAAI
   b. A Stake in the Outcome
   c. A4e
   d. Apprenticeship

2. An _____ is a mostly hierarchical concept of subordination of entities that collaborate and contribute to serve one common aim.

   Organizations are a variant of clustered entities. The structure of an organization is usually set up in many a styles, dependent on their objectives and ambience.

   a. Organizational structure
   b. Informal organization
   c. Organizational development
   d. Open shop

3. _____ is an increasingly broadening term with which an organization, or other human system describes the combination of traditionally administrative personnel functions with acquisition and application of skills, knowledge and experience, Employee Relations and resource planning at various levels. The field draws upon concepts developed in Industrial/Organizational Psychology and System Theory. _____ has at least two related interpretations depending on context. The original usage derives from political economy and economics, where it was traditionally called labor, one of four factors of production although this perspective is changing as a function of new and ongoing research into more strategic approaches at national levels. This first usage is used more in terms of '_____ development', and can go beyond just organizations to the level of nations. The more traditional usage within corporations and businesses refers to the individuals within a firm or agency, and to the portion of the organization that deals with hiring, firing, training, and other personnel issues, typically referred to as `_____ management'.
   a. Bradford Factor
   b. Human resource management
   c. Progressive discipline
   d. Human resources

4. _____ is a contract between two parties, one being the employer and the other being the employee. An employee may be defined as: 'A person in the service of another under any contract of hire, express or implied, oral or written, where the employer has the power or right to control and direct the employee in the material details of how the work is to be performed.' Black's Law Dictionary page 471 (5th ed. 1979.)
   a. Exit interview
   b. Employment counsellor
   c. Employment
   d. Employment rate

5. The _____ was a period in the late 18th and early 19th centuries when major changes in agriculture, manufacturing, mining, and transportation had a profound effect on the socioeconomic and cultural conditions in Britain. The changes subsequently spread throughout Europe, North America, and eventually the world. The onset of the _____ marked a major turning point in human society; almost every aspect of daily life was eventually influenced in some way.
   a. Affiliation
   b. Industrial Revolution
   c. Abraham Harold Maslow
   d. Adam Smith

Chapter 6. Human Resources Management in Organized Delivery Systems

6. _____ is a theory of management that analyzes and synthesizes workflows, with the objective of improving labour productivity. The core ideas of the theory were developed by Frederick Winslow Taylor in the 1880s and 1890s, and were first published in his monographs, Shop Management and The Principles of _____ Taylor believed that decisions based upon tradition and rules of thumb should be replaced by precise procedures developed after careful study of an individual at work.

   a. Capacity planning
   b. Value engineering
   c. Master production schedule
   d. Scientific management

7. _____, is the discipline of using scientific research-based principles, strategies, and other analytical methods, such as mathematical modeling to improve any organization's ability to enact rational, meaningful business management decisions.

   a. Trustee
   b. Workflow
   c. Cross ownership
   d. Management science

8. Human resource management (HRM) is the strategic and coherent approach to the management of an organisation's most valued assets - the people working there who individually and collectively contribute to the achievement of the objectives of the business. The terms 'human resource management' and 'human resources' (HR) have largely replaced the term '_____' as a description of the processes involved in managing people in organizations. In simple sense, HRM means employing people, developing their resources, utilizing, maintaining and compensating their services in tune with the job and organizational requirement.

   a. Progressive discipline
   b. Salary
   c. Personnel management
   d. Human resources

9. _____ is the process of systematically determining a relative value of jobs in an organisation. In all cases the idea is to evaluate the job, not the person doing it.

   - Job Ranking is the most simple form. Basically you just order the jobs according to perceived seniority. It's easy in a small organization, but get exponentially difficult with lots of different jobs.

   - Pair Comparison introduces more rigour by comparing jobs in pairs, but really it's a more structured way of building a basic rank order.

   - Benchmarking or slotting sets up certain jobs that are analysed in detail. These are then used for comparison to slot jobs against these benchmarks.

   a. 33 Strategies of War
   b. 1990 Clean Air Act
   c. 28-hour day
   d. Job evaluation

10. _____ is an advertisement in which a particular product specifically mentions a competitor by name for the express purpose of showing why the competitor is inferior to the product naming it.

This should not be confused with parody advertisements, where a fictional product is being advertised for the purpose of poking fun at the particular advertisement, nor should it be confused with the use of a coined brand name for the purpose of comparing the product without actually naming an actual competitor. ('Wikipedia tastes better and is less filling than the Encyclopedia Galactica.')

Chapter 6. Human Resources Management in Organized Delivery Systems

In the 1980s, during what has been referred to as the cola wars, soft-drink manufacturer Pepsi ran a series of advertisements where people, caught on hidden camera, in a blind taste test, chose Pepsi over rival Coca-Cola.

   a. 28-hour day
   c. 33 Strategies of War

   b. 1990 Clean Air Act
   d. Comparative advertising

11. A _____ is a compensation, usually financial, received by a worker in exchange for their labor.

Compensation in terms of _____s is given to worker and compensation in terms of salary is given to employees. Compensation is a monetary benefits given to employees in returns of the services provided by them.

   a. Performance-related pay
   c. Wage

   b. Profit-sharing agreement
   d. State Compensation Insurance Fund

12. The _____ is the labour pool in employment. It is generally used to describe those working for a single company or industry, but can also apply to a geographic region like a city, country, state, etc. The term generally excludes the employers or management, and implies those involved in manual labour.

   a. Division of labour
   c. Workforce

   b. Work-life balance
   d. Pink-collar worker

13. _____, known in the United States as antitrust law, has three main elements:

- prohibiting agreements or practices that restrict free trading and competition between business entities. This includes in particular the repression of cartels.
- banning abusive behavior by a firm dominating a market, or anti-competitive practices that tend to lead to such a dominant position. Practices controlled in this way may include predatory pricing, tying, price gouging, refusal to deal, and many others.
- supervising the mergers and acquisitions of large corporations, including some joint ventures. Transactions that are considered to threaten the competitive process can be prohibited altogether, or approved subject to 'remedies' such as an obligation to divest part of the merged business or to offer licenses or access to facilities to enable other businesses to continue competing.

The substance and practice of _____ varies from jurisdiction to jurisdiction. Protecting the interests of consumers (consumer welfare) and ensuring that entrepreneurs have an opportunity to compete in the market economy are often treated as important objectives. _____ is closely connected with law on deregulation of access to markets, state aids and subsidies, the privatization of state owned assets and the establishment of independent sector regulators. In recent decades, _____ has been viewed as a way to provide better public services.

   a. Federal Employers Liability Act
   c. Competition law

   b. Rulemaking
   d. Right to Financial Privacy Act

14. A _____ is a form of periodic payment from an employer to an employee, which may be specified in an employment contract. It is contrasted with piece wages, where each job, hour or other unit is paid separately, rather than on a periodic basis.

Chapter 6. Human Resources Management in Organized Delivery Systems 37

From the point of a view of running a business, _____ can also be viewed as the cost of acquiring human resources for running operations, and is then termed personnel expense or _____ expense.

a. Training and development
b. Human resources
c. Human resource management
d. Salary

15. The field of _____ looks at the relationship between management and workers, particularly groups of workers represented by a union.

_____ is an important factor in analyzing 'varieties of capitalism', such as neocorporatism, social democracy, and neoliberalism

a. Overtime
b. Industrial relations
c. Organizational effectiveness
d. Informal organization

16. A _____ is a list of the general tasks and responsibilities of a position. Typically, it also includes to whom the position reports, specifications such as the qualifications needed by the person in the job, salary range for the position, etc. A _____ is usually developed by conducting a job analysis, which includes examining the tasks and sequences of tasks necessary to perform the job.

a. Recruitment Process Insourcing
b. Recruitment advertising
c. Recruitment
d. Job description

17. _____ refers to the process of screening, and selecting qualified people for a job at an organization or firm mid- and large-size organizations and companies often retain professional recruiters or outsource some of the process to _____ agencies. External _____ is the process of attracting and selecting employees from outside the organization.

The _____ industry has four main types of agencies: employment agencies, _____ websites and job search engines, 'headhunters' for executive and professional _____, and in-house _____.

a. Recruitment Process Outsourcing
b. Referral recruitment
c. Labour hire
d. Recruitment

18. _____ is a form of communication that typically attempts to persuade potential customers to purchase or to consume more of a particular brand of product or service. 'While now central to the contemporary global economy and the reproduction of global production networks, it is only quite recently that _____ has been more than a marginal influence on patterns of sales and production. The formation of modern _____ was intimately bound up with the emergence of new forms of monopoly capitalism around the end of the 19th and beginning of the 20th century as one element in corporate strategies to create, organize and where possible control markets, especially for mass produced consumer goods.

a. A4e
b. A Stake in the Outcome
c. AAAI
d. Advertising

19.

The terms _____ and positive action refer to policies that take race, ethnicity, or gender into consideration in an attempt to promote equal opportunity. The focus of such policies ranges from employment and education to public contracting and health programs. The impetus towards _____ is twofold: to maximize diversity in all levels of society, along with its presumed benefits, and to redress perceived disadvantages due to overt, institutional, or involuntary discrimination.

   a. Affiliation
   c. Abraham Harold Maslow
   b. Affirmative action
   d. Adam Smith

20. An _____ details guidelines, expectations and procedures of a business or company to its employees.

_____s are given to employees on one of the first days of his/her job, in order to acquaint them with their new company and its policies.

Chapter 6. Human Resources Management in Organized Delivery Systems 39

While it often varies from business to business, specific areas that an _____ may address include:

- A welcome statement, which may also briefly describe the company's history, reasons for its success and how the employee can contribute to future successes. It may also include a mission statement, or a statement about a business' goals and objectives.
- Orientation procedures. This usually involves providing a human resources manager or other designated employee completed income tax withholding forms, providing proof of identity and eligibility for employment (in accordance with the Immigration Reform and Control Act of 1986), proof of a completed drug test (by a designated medical center) and other required forms.
- Definitions of full- and part-time employment, and benefits each classification receives. In addition, this area also describes timekeeping procedures (such as defining a 'work week'.) This area may also include information about daily breaks (for lunch and rest.)
- Information about employee pay and benefits (such as vacation and insurance.) Usually, new employees are awarded some benefits, plus additional rewards (such as enrollment in a 401K retirement account program, additional vacation and pay raises) after having worked for a company for a certain period of time. These are spelled out in this section.
- Expectations about conduct and discipline policies. These sections include conduct policies for such areas as sexual harassment, alcohol and drug use, and attendance; plus, grounds for dismissal (i.e., getting fired) and due process. This area may also include information about filing grievances with supervisors and/or co-workers, and communicating work-related issues with supervisors and/or company managers.
- Guidelines for employee performance reviews (such as how and when they are conducted.)
- Policies for promotion or demotion to a certain position.
- Rules concerning mail; use of the telephone, company equipment, Internet and e-mail; and employee use of motor vehicles for job assignments.
- Procedures on handling on-the-job accidents, such as those that result in injury.
- How an employee may voluntarily terminate his job (through retirement or resignation), and exit interviews.
- A requirement that employees keep certain business information confidential. This area usually includes information about releasing employee records and information, as well as who may retrieve and inspect the information.

If the employer is covered by the Family and Medical Leave Act of 1993 - generally 50 or more employees - a handbook must have information about FMLA.

New employees are usually required to sign a form stating they have read and understand the information, and accept the terms of the _____.

a. Underemployment
b. Informational interview
c. Employment
d. Employee handbook

21. In a human resources context, _____ or labor _____ is the rate at which an employer gains and loses employees. Simple ways to describe it are 'how long employees tend to stay' or 'the rate of traffic through the revolving door.' _____ is measured for individual companies and for their industry as a whole. If an employer is said to have a high _____ relative to its competitors, it means that employees of that company have a shorter average tenure than those of other companies in the same industry.

a. Turnover
b. Continuous
c. Career portfolios
d. Ten year occupational employment projection

22. _____ involves establishing specific, measurable and time-targeted objectives. Work on the theory of goal-setting suggests that it's an effective tool for making progress by ensuring that participants in a group with a common goal are clearly aware of what is expected from them if an objective is to be achieved. On a personal level, setting goals is a process that allows people to specify then work towards their own objectives - most commonly with financial or career-based goals.

a. Resource-based view
b. Goal setting
c. Catfish effect
d. Digital strategy

23. A _____ is a set of categories designed to elicit information about a quantitative or a qualitative attribute. In the social sciences, common examples are the Likert scale and 1-10 _____s in which a person selects the number which is considered to reflect the perceived quality of a product.

A _____ is an instrument that requires the rater to assign the rated object that have numerals assigned to them.

a. Polytomous Rasch model
b. Thurstone scale
c. Spearman-Brown prediction formula
d. Rating scale

24. _____ is best described as the process from which managers learn and improve their skills not only to benefit themselves but also their employing organizations.

In organisational development (OD), the effectiveness of management is recognised as one of the determinants of organisational success. Therefore, investment in _____ can have a direct economic benefit to the organization.

a. Management development
b. Senior management
c. Fix it twice
d. Job enrichment

25. The _____ is a 1935 United States federal law that limits the means with which employers may react to workers in the private sector that organize labor unions, engage in collective bargaining, and take part in strikes and other forms of concerted activity in support of their demands. The Act does not, on the other hand, cover those workers who are covered by the Railway Labor Act, agricultural employees, domestic employees, supervisors, independent contractors and some close relatives of individual employers.

It was in a context of severe economic troubles that the Wagner Act came into effect.

a. 1990 Clean Air Act
b. 33 Strategies of War
c. 28-hour day
d. National Labor Relations Act

26. _____ is the practice of empowering employees to participate in organizational decision making. This practice grew out of the human relations movement in the 1920s, and is based on some of the principles discovered by scholars doing research in management and organization studies, such as the Hawthorne Effect.

While senior managers still retain final decision making authority when _____ is practiced, employees are encouraged to voice their opinions about their working conditions in a safe environment, protected from the potential defensiveness of middle managers who they might criticize.

a. Human Relations Movement
b. Job satisfaction
c. Participatory management
d. Management process

27. A _____ is a volunteer group composed of workers (or even students), usually under the leadership of their supervisor (but they can elect a team leader), who are trained to identify, analyse and solve work-related problems and present their solutions to management in order to improve the performance of the organization, and motivate and enrich the work of employees. When matured, true _____s become self-managing, having gained the confidence of management. _____s are an alternative to the dehumanising concept of the Division of Labour, where workers or individuals are treated like robots.

a. Connectionist expert systems
b. Certified in Production and Inventory Management
c. Competency-based job descriptions
d. Quality circle

28. _____, a form of alternative dispute resolution (ADR), is a legal technique for the resolution of disputes outside the courts, wherein the parties to a dispute refer it to one or more persons (the 'arbitrators', 'arbiters' or 'arbitral tribunal'), by whose decision (the 'award') they agree to be bound. It is a settlement technique in which a third party reviews the case and imposes a decision that is legally binding for both sides. Other forms of ADR include mediation (a form of settlement negotiation facilitated by a neutral third party) and non-binding resolution by experts.

a. Arbitration
b. A4e
c. A Stake in the Outcome
d. AAAI

29. In general, a _____ is an arrangement to provide people with an income when they are no longer earning a regular income from employment.

The terms retirement plan or superannuation refer to a _____ granted upon retirement. Retirement plans may be set up by employers, insurance companies, the government or other institutions such as employer associations or trade unions.

a. State Compensation Insurance Fund
b. Pension
c. Wage
d. Pension insurance contract

30. _____ and benefits in kind are various non-wage compensations provided to employees in addition to their normal wages or salaries. Where an employee exchanges (cash) wages for some other form of benefit, this is generally referred to as a 'salary sacrifice' arrangement. In most countries, most kinds of _____ are taxable to at least some degree.

a. Interactive Accommodation Process
b. A4e
c. A Stake in the Outcome
d. Employee benefits

Chapter 6. Human Resources Management in Organized Delivery Systems

31. _____ is an organization's process of defining its strategy and making decisions on allocating its resources to pursue this strategy, including its capital and people. Various business analysis techniques can be used in _____, including SWOT analysis (Strengths, Weaknesses, Opportunities, and Threats) and PEST analysis (Political, Economic, Social, and Technological analysis) or STEER analysis involving Socio-cultural, Technological, Economic, Ecological, and Regulatory factors and EPISTEL (Environment, Political, Informatic, Social, Technological, Economic and Legal)

_____ is the formal consideration of an organization's future course. All _____ deals with at least one of three key questions:

1. 'What do we do?'
2. 'For whom do we do it?'
3. 'How do we excel?'

In business _____, the third question is better phrased 'How can we beat or avoid competition?'. (Bradford and Duncan, page 1.)

a. 1990 Clean Air Act
b. Strategic planning
c. 33 Strategies of War
d. 28-hour day

32. A _____ or chief executive is one of the highest-ranking corporate officer (executive) or administrator in charge of total management. An individual selected as President and _____ of a corporation, company, organization, or agency, reports to the board of directors. In internal communication and press releases, many companies capitalize the term and those of other high positions, even when they are not proper nouns.

a. Chief brand officer
b. Purchasing manager
c. Financial analyst
d. Chief executive officer

33. While _____ literally refers to a person responsible for the performance of duties involved in running an organization, the exact meaning of the role is variable, depending on the organization.

While there is no clear line between executive or principal and inferior officers, principal officers are high-level officials in the executive branch of U.S. government such as department heads of independent agencies. In Humphrey's Executor v. United States, 295 U.S. 602 (1935), the Court distinguished between _____s and quasi-legislative or quasi-judicial officers by stating that the former serve at the pleasure of the President and may be removed at his discretion.

a. Australian Fair Pay and Conditions Standard
b. Executive officer
c. Easement
d. Unreported employment

34. _____ is the strategic and coherent approach to the management of an organisation's most valued assets - the people working there who individually and collectively contribute to the achievement of the objectives of the business. The terms '_____' and 'human resources' (HR) have largely replaced the term 'personnel management' as a description of the processes involved in managing people in organizations. In simple sense, _____ means employing people, developing their resources, utilizing, maintaining and compensating their services in tune with the job and organizational requirement.

a. Human resource management
b. Progressive discipline
c. Job knowledge
d. Revolving door syndrome

35. The American Federation of Labor and Congress of Industrial Organizations, commonly _____, is a national trade union center, the largest federation of unions in the United States, made up of 65 national and international unions (including Canadian), together representing more than 10 million workers. It was formed in 1955 when the AFL and the CIO merged after a long estrangement. From 1955 until 2005, the _____'s member unions represented nearly all unionized workers in the United States.
   a. United Mine Workers
   b. A Stake in the Outcome
   c. A4e
   d. AFL-CIO

36. _____ is the process of estimation in unknown situations. Prediction is a similar, but more general term. Both can refer to estimation of time series, cross-sectional or longitudinal data.
   a. 28-hour day
   b. 33 Strategies of War
   c. 1990 Clean Air Act
   d. Forecasting

37. In economics, business, retail, and accounting, a _____ is the value of money that has been used up to produce something, and hence is not available for use anymore. In economics, a _____ is an alternative that is given up as a result of a decision. In business, the _____ may be one of acquisition, in which case the amount of money expended to acquire it is counted as _____.
   a. Cost allocation
   b. Fixed costs
   c. Cost overrun
   d. Cost

38. A chief executive officer (_____) or chief executive is one of the highest-ranking corporate officer (executive) or administrator in charge of total management. An individual selected as President and _____ of a corporation, company, organization, or agency, reports to the board of directors. In internal communication and press releases, many companies capitalize the term and those of other high positions, even when they are not proper nouns.
   a. Director of communications
   b. Portfolio manager
   c. Chief executive officer
   d. CEO

39. An _____ is the negative aspects of human activity on the biophysical environment. Environmentalism, a social and environmental movement that started in the 1960s, focuses on addressing _____s through advocacy, education and activism.

Major current _____s are climate change, pollution and resource depletion.

   a. A4e
   b. Environmental issue
   c. A Stake in the Outcome
   d. AAAI

Chapter 7. Labor and Employment Laws Applicable to Organized Delivery Systems

1. _____ is an advertisement in which a particular product specifically mentions a competitor by name for the express purpose of showing why the competitor is inferior to the product naming it.

This should not be confused with parody advertisements, where a fictional product is being advertised for the purpose of poking fun at the particular advertisement, nor should it be confused with the use of a coined brand name for the purpose of comparing the product without actually naming an actual competitor. ('Wikipedia tastes better and is less filling than the Encyclopedia Galactica.')

In the 1980s, during what has been referred to as the cola wars, soft-drink manufacturer Pepsi ran a series of advertisements where people, caught on hidden camera, in a blind taste test, chose Pepsi over rival Coca-Cola.

- a. Comparative advertising
- b. 28-hour day
- c. 33 Strategies of War
- d. 1990 Clean Air Act

2. _____, known in the United States as antitrust law, has three main elements:

- prohibiting agreements or practices that restrict free trading and competition between business entities. This includes in particular the repression of cartels.
- banning abusive behavior by a firm dominating a market, or anti-competitive practices that tend to lead to such a dominant position. Practices controlled in this way may include predatory pricing, tying, price gouging, refusal to deal, and many others.
- supervising the mergers and acquisitions of large corporations, including some joint ventures. Transactions that are considered to threaten the competitive process can be prohibited altogether, or approved subject to 'remedies' such as an obligation to divest part of the merged business or to offer licenses or access to facilities to enable other businesses to continue competing.

The substance and practice of _____ varies from jurisdiction to jurisdiction. Protecting the interests of consumers (consumer welfare) and ensuring that entrepreneurs have an opportunity to compete in the market economy are often treated as important objectives. _____ is closely connected with law on deregulation of access to markets, state aids and subsidies, the privatization of state owned assets and the establishment of independent sector regulators. In recent decades, _____ has been viewed as a way to provide better public services.

- a. Right to Financial Privacy Act
- b. Federal Employers Liability Act
- c. Rulemaking
- d. Competition law

3. _____ is the process of estimation in unknown situations. Prediction is a similar, but more general term. Both can refer to estimation of time series, cross-sectional or longitudinal data.
- a. 28-hour day
- b. 33 Strategies of War
- c. 1990 Clean Air Act
- d. Forecasting

4. The field of _____ looks at the relationship between management and workers, particularly groups of workers represented by a union.

_____ is an important factor in analyzing 'varieties of capitalism', such as neocorporatism, social democracy, and neoliberalism

Chapter 7. Labor and Employment Laws Applicable to Organized Delivery Systems

a. Informal organization
b. Overtime
c. Organizational effectiveness
d. Industrial relations

5. _____ is the body of laws, administrative rulings, and precedents which address the legal rights of, and restrictions on, working people and their organizations. As such, it mediates many aspects of the relationship between trade unions, employers and employees. In Canada, employment laws related to unionized workplaces are differentiated from those relating to particular individuals.

a. Labor law
b. Shift work
c. Trade union
d. Four-day week

6. The _____ is a 1935 United States federal law that limits the means with which employers may react to workers in the private sector that organize labor unions, engage in collective bargaining, and take part in strikes and other forms of concerted activity in support of their demands. The Act does not, on the other hand, cover those workers who are covered by the Railway Labor Act, agricultural employees, domestic employees, supervisors, independent contractors and some close relatives of individual employers.

It was in a context of severe economic troubles that the Wagner Act came into effect.

a. National Labor Relations Act
b. 33 Strategies of War
c. 1990 Clean Air Act
d. 28-hour day

7. _____ is a contract between two parties, one being the employer and the other being the employee. An employee may be defined as: 'A person in the service of another under any contract of hire, express or implied, oral or written, where the employer has the power or right to control and direct the employee in the material details of how the work is to be performed.' Black's Law Dictionary page 471 (5th ed. 1979.)

a. Employment
b. Employment rate
c. Employment counsellor
d. Exit interview

8. _____, a form of alternative dispute resolution (ADR), is a legal technique for the resolution of disputes outside the courts, wherein the parties to a dispute refer it to one or more persons (the 'arbitrators', 'arbiters' or 'arbitral tribunal'), by whose decision (the 'award') they agree to be bound. It is a settlement technique in which a third party reviews the case and imposes a decision that is legally binding for both sides. Other forms of ADR include mediation (a form of settlement negotiation facilitated by a neutral third party) and non-binding resolution by experts.

a. Arbitration
b. A4e
c. AAAI
d. A Stake in the Outcome

9. In organized labor, _____ is the method whereby workers organize together (usually in unions) to meet, converse, and negotiate upon the work conditions with their employers normally resulting in a written contract setting forth the wages, hours, and other conditions to be observed for a stipulated period.It is the practice in which union and company representatives meet to negotiate a new labor contract. In various national labor and employment law contexts, the term _____ takes on a more specific legal meaning. In a broad sense, however, it is the coming together of workers to negotiate their employment.

a. Collective bargaining
b. Labor rights
c. Labour law
d. Paid time off

10. _____ is the concept of a person or group of people being in charge or in command of another person or group. This control is often granted to the senior person(s) due to experience or length of service in a given position, but it is not uncommon for a senior person(s) to have less experience or length of service than their subordinates.

More generally, '_____' can be a description of an individual's experience or length of service, and can thus be used to differentiate between individuals of otherwise equivalent status without placing them in a hierarchy of direct authority.

    a. 28-hour day
    b. 1990 Clean Air Act
    c. 33 Strategies of War
    d. Seniority

11. A _____ exists when an employee experiences workplace harassment and fears going to work because of the offensive, intimidating religion, sex, national origin, age, disability, veteran status, or, in some jurisdictions, sexual orientation, political affiliation, citizenship status, marital status, or personal appearance. _____ is also one of the two legal categories of sexual harassment.

The anti-discrimination statutes governing _____ are not a general civility code.

    a. Contrat nouvelle embauche
    b. Flextime
    c. Financial Security Law of France
    d. Hostile work environment

12. _____ indicates a more-or-less equal exchange or substitution of goods or services. English speakers often use the term to mean 'a favour for a favour' and the phrases with almost identical meaning include: 'what for what,' 'give and take,' 'tit for tat', 'this for that', and 'you scratch my back, and I'll scratch yours'.

In legal usage, _____ indicates that an item or a service has been traded in return for something of value, usually when the propriety or equity of the transaction is in question.

    a. 28-hour day
    b. Quid pro quo
    c. 33 Strategies of War
    d. 1990 Clean Air Act

13. _____ is unwelcome harassment of a sexual nature, or based upon the receiving party's sex or gender. In some contexts or circumstances, _____ may be illegal. It includes a range of behavior from seemingly mild transgressions and annoyances to actual sexual abuse or sexual assault.

    a. Hypernorms
    b. 1990 Clean Air Act
    c. 28-hour day
    d. Sexual harassment

14. The _____ is a United States labor law allowing an employee to take unpaid leave due to a serious health condition that makes the employee unable to perform his job or to care for a sick family member or to care for a new son or daughter (including by birth, adoption or foster care.) The bill was among the first signed into law by President Bill Clinton in his first term.

    a. Sarbanes-Oxley Act of 2002
    b. Family and Medical Leave Act of 1993
    c. Contributory negligence
    d. Harvester Judgment

Chapter 7. Labor and Employment Laws Applicable to Organized Delivery Systems

15. The _____ of 1967, Pub. L. No. 90-202, 81 Stat. 602 (Dec. 15, 1967), codified as Chapter 14 of Title 29 of the United States Code, 29 U.S.C. § 621 through 29 U.S.C. § 634 (ADEA), prohibits employment discrimination against persons 40 years of age or older in the United States). The law also sets standards for pensions and benefits provided by employers and requires that information about the needs of older workers be provided to the general public.
   a. Unemployment and Farm Relief Act
   b. Age Discrimination in Employment Act
   c. Undue hardship
   d. Extra time

16.

The terms _____ and positive action refer to policies that take race, ethnicity, or gender into consideration in an attempt to promote equal opportunity. The focus of such policies ranges from employment and education to public contracting and health programs. The impetus towards _____ is twofold: to maximize diversity in all levels of society, along with its presumed benefits, and to redress perceived disadvantages due to overt, institutional, or involuntary discrimination.

   a. Affiliation
   b. Affirmative action
   c. Abraham Harold Maslow
   d. Adam Smith

17. The _____ is an American federal law which allows people who are not affiliated with the government to file actions against federal contractors claiming fraud against the government. The act of filing such actions is informally called 'whistleblowing.' Persons filing under the Act stand to receive a portion (usually about 15-25 percent) of any recovered damages.
   a. Personal Responsibility and Work Opportunity Reconciliation Act
   b. Bennett Amendment
   c. Chrapliwy v. Uniroyal
   d. False Claims Act

18. The _____ is the labour pool in employment. It is generally used to describe those working for a single company or industry, but can also apply to a geographic region like a city, country, state, etc. The term generally excludes the employers or management, and implies those involved in manual labour.
   a. Pink-collar worker
   b. Division of labour
   c. Work-life balance
   d. Workforce

19. A _____ or background investigation is the process of looking up and compiling criminal records, commercial records and financial records (in certain instances such as employment screening) of an individual.

_____s are often requested by employers on job candidates, especially on candidates seeking a position that requires high security or a position of trust, such as in a school, hospital, financial institution, airport, and government (including law enforcement and military.) These checks are traditionally administered by a government agency for a nominal fee, but can also be administered by private companies.

   a. Time and attendance
   b. Labour productivity
   c. Malcolm Baldrige National Quality Award
   d. Background check

20. A _____ is a person who alleges misconduct. More complex definitions may be used, but the issue is that the _____ usually faces reprisal. The misconduct may be classified in many ways; for example, a violation of a law, rule, regulation and/or a direct threat to public interest, such as fraud, health/safety violations, and corruption.

a. Whistleblower
b. 28-hour day
c. 1990 Clean Air Act
d. 33 Strategies of War

21. The U.S. _____ of 1988 ('_____') generally prevents employers from using lie detector tests, either for pre-employment screening or during the course of employment, with certain exemptions. Employers generally may not require or request any employee or job applicant to take a lie detector test, or discharge, discipline, or discriminate against an employee or job applicant for refusing to take a test or for exercising other rights under the Act. In addition, employers are required to display a poster in the workplace explaining the _____ for their employees.
   a. Employee Polygraph Protection Act
   b. A4e
   c. AAAI
   d. A Stake in the Outcome

22. The _____ of 1938 (_____, ch. 676, 52 Stat. 1060, June 25, 1938, 29 U.S.C. ch.8), also called the Wages and Hours Bill, is United States federal law that applies to employees engaged in interstate commerce or employed by an enterprise engaged in commerce or in the production of goods for commerce, unless the employer can claim an exemption from coverage. The _____ established a national minimum wage, guaranteed time and a half for overtime in certain jobs, and prohibited most employment of minors in 'oppressive child labor,' a term defined in the statute.
   a. Joint venture
   b. Board of directors
   c. Family and Medical Leave Act of 1993
   d. Fair Labor Standards Act

23. _____ are conventions, treaties and recommendations designed to eliminate unjust and inhumane labour practices. The primary inernational agency charged with developing such standards is the International Labour Organization (ILO.) Established in 1919, the ILO advocates international standards as essential for the eradication of labour conditions involving 'injustice, hardship and privation'.
   a. Airbus Industrie
   b. Airbus SAS
   c. Anaconda Copper
   d. International labour standards

24. _____ is the temporary suspension or permanent termination of employment of an employee or (more commonly) a group of employees for business reasons, such as the decision that certain positions are no longer necessary or a business slow-down or interruption in work. Originally the term '_____' referred exclusively to a temporary interruption in work, as when factory work cyclically falls off. However, in recent times the term can also refer to the permanent elimination of a position.
   a. Layoff
   b. Termination of employment
   c. Retirement
   d. Wrongful dismissal

25. _____ is the process of learning a new skill or trade, often in response to a change in the economic environment. Generally it reflects changes in profession choice rather than an 'upward' movement in the same field.

There is some controversy surrounding the use of _____ to offset economic changes caused by free trade and automation.

   a. Krauthammer
   b. Suspension training
   c. Compliance Training
   d. Retraining

26. The _____ is a United States labor law which protects employees, their families, and communities by requiring most employers with 100 or more employees to provide sixty- (60) calendar-day advance notification of plant closings and mass layoffs of employees. It was enacted in 1989.

Chapter 7. Labor and Employment Laws Applicable to Organized Delivery Systems

Employees entitled to notice under the _____ include managers and supervisors, hourly wage, and salaried workers.

a. Worker Adjustment and Retraining Notification Act
b. Robinson-Patman Act
c. Non-disclosure agreement
d. Leave of absence

27. A _____ is a compensation, usually financial, received by a worker in exchange for their labor.

Compensation in terms of _____s is given to worker and compensation in terms of salary is given to employees. Compensation is a monetary benefits given to employees in returns of the services provided by them.

a. Profit-sharing agreement
b. Wage
c. Performance-related pay
d. State Compensation Insurance Fund

28. _____ is the amount of time someone works beyond normal working hours. Normal hours may be determined in several ways:

- by custom (what is considered healthy or reasonable by society),
- by practices of a given trade or profession,
- by legislation,
- by agreement between employers and workers or their representatives.

Most nations have _____ laws designed to dissuade or prevent employers from forcing their employees to work excessively long hours. These laws may take into account other considerations than the humanitarian, such as increasing the overall level of employment in the economy. One common approach to regulating _____ is to require employers to pay workers at a higher hourly rate for _____ work.

a. Organizational effectiveness
b. Organizational structure
c. Industrial relations
d. Overtime

29. A _____ is the lowest hourly, daily or monthly wage that employers may legally pay to employees or workers. Equivalently, it is the lowest wage at which workers may sell their labor. Although _____ laws are in effect in a great many jurisdictions, there are differences of opinion about the benefits and drawbacks of a _____.

a. Value added
b. Rehn-Meidner Model
c. Minimum Wage
d. Deregulation

30. _____ is one of the managerial functions like planning, organizing, staffing and directing. It is an important function because it helps to check the errors and to take the corrective action so that deviation from standards are minimized and stated goals of the organization are achieved in desired manner. According to modern concepts, _____ is a foreseeing action whereas earlier concept of _____ was used only when errors were detected. _____ in management means setting standards, measuring actual performance and taking corrective action.

a. Schedule of reinforcement
b. Turnover
c. Decision tree pruning
d. Control

31. _____ is an arrangement in which a portion of an employee's income is paid out at a date after which that income is actually earned. Examples of _____ include pensions, retirement plans, and stock options. The primary benefit of most _____ is the deferral of tax to the date(s) at which the employee actually receives the income.
   a. Deferred compensation
   b. Market value
   c. Restructuring
   d. Novated lease

32. In economics, a _____ is a type of pension plan in which an employer promises a specified monthly benefit on retirement that is predetermined by a formula based on the employee's earnings history, tenure of service and age, rather than depending on investment returns. It is 'defined' in the sense that the formula for computing the employer's contribution is known in advance. In the United States, 26 U.S.C.
   a. Defined benefit pension plan
   b. Reservation wage
   c. Capital costs
   d. Buffer stock

33. The _____ (Pub.L. 93-406, 88 Stat. 829, enacted September 2, 1974) is an American federal statute that establishes minimum standards for pension plans in private industry and provides for extensive rules on the federal income tax effects of transactions associated with employee benefit plans.
   a. A Stake in the Outcome
   b. AAAI
   c. Employee Retirement Income Security Act of 1974
   d. A4e

34. _____ is the point where a person stops employment completely. A person may also semi-retire and keep some sort of _____ job, out of choice rather than necessity. This usually happens upon reaching a determined age, when physical conditions don't allow the person to work any more (by illness or accident), or even for personal choice (usually in the presence of an adequate pension or personal savings.)
   a. Wrongful dismissal
   b. Termination of employment
   c. Severance package
   d. Retirement

35. The terms _____ or superannuation refer to a pension granted upon retirement. _____s may be set up by employers, insurance companies, the government or other institutions such as employer associations or trade unions. Called _____s in the USA, they are more commonly known as pension schemes in the UK and Ireland and superannuation plans in Australia.
   a. Real wage
   b. Retirement plan
   c. Salary calculator
   d. Wage

36. _____ and benefits in kind are various non-wage compensations provided to employees in addition to their normal wages or salaries. Where an employee exchanges (cash) wages for some other form of benefit, this is generally referred to as a 'salary sacrifice' arrangement. In most countries, most kinds of _____ are taxable to at least some degree.
   a. A Stake in the Outcome
   b. Interactive Accommodation Process
   c. A4e
   d. Employee benefits

37. In general, a _____ is an arrangement to provide people with an income when they are no longer earning a regular income from employment.

The terms retirement plan or superannuation refer to a _____ granted upon retirement. Retirement plans may be set up by employers, insurance companies, the government or other institutions such as employer associations or trade unions.

Chapter 7. Labor and Employment Laws Applicable to Organized Delivery Systems

a. Wage
b. Pension
c. Pension insurance contract
d. State Compensation Insurance Fund

38. An _____ is the negative aspects of human activity on the biophysical environment. Environmentalism, a social and environmental movement that started in the 1960s, focuses on addressing _____s through advocacy, education and activism.

Major current _____s are climate change, pollution and resource depletion.

a. A4e
b. AAAI
c. A Stake in the Outcome
d. Environmental issue

39. Employees typically must relinquish some of their _____, but how much they must do so can be a contentious issue. Employers might choose to monitor employees activities using surveillance cameras, or may wish to record employees activities while using company owned computers or telephones.

The EU Directive 95/46/EC on the protection of individuals with regard to the processing of personal data and on the free movement of such data limits and regulates the collection of personal information on individuals, including workers.

a. Complement
b. Privacy while at the workplace
c. Procter ' Gamble
d. Job security through obscurity

40. _____ is a cross-disciplinary area concerned with protecting the safety, health and welfare of people engaged in work or employment. The goal of all _____ programs is to foster a work free safe environment. As a secondary effect, it may also protect co-workers, family members, employers, customers, suppliers, nearby communities, and other members of the public who are impacted by the workplace environment.

a. Occupational Safety and Health
b. AAAI
c. A Stake in the Outcome
d. A4e

41. The _____ is the primary federal law which governs occupational health and safety in the private sector and federal government in the United States. It was enacted by Congress in 1970 and was signed by President Richard Nixon on December 29, 1970. Its main goal is to ensure that employers provide employees with an environment free from recognized hazards, such as exposure to toxic chemicals, excessive noise levels, mechanical dangers, heat or cold stress, or unsanitary conditions.

a. United States Department of Justice
b. Unemployment and Farm Relief Act
c. Unemployment Action Center
d. Occupational Safety and Health Act

42. _____ is a category of management responsibility in places of employment.

Chapter 7. Labor and Employment Laws Applicable to Organized Delivery Systems

To ensure the safety and health of workers, managers establish a focus on safety that can include elements such as:

- management leadership and commitment
- employee engagement
- accountability
- ensuring all task are carried out safely and effeintly
- safety programs, policies, and plans
- safety processes, procedures, and practices
- safety goals and objectives
- safety inspections for workplace hazards
- safety program audits
- safety tracking ' metrics
- hazard identification and control
- safety committees to promote employee involvement
- safety education and training
- safety communications to maintain a high level of awareness on safety

Data from 2003

In most countries males comprise the vast majority of workplace fatalities. In the EU as a whole, 94% of death were of males.

The Bureau of Labor Statistics of the United States Department of Labor compiles information about workplace fatalities in the United States.

a. 33 Strategies of War
b. 28-hour day
c. 1990 Clean Air Act
d. Workplace safety

43. _____ is one of the four elements of marketing mix. An organization or set of organizations (go-betweens) involved in the process of making a product or service available for use or consumption by a consumer or business user.

The other three parts of the marketing mix are product, pricing, and promotion.

a. Missing completely at random
b. Distribution
c. Job creation programs
d. Matching theory

44. An _____ is a natural person, business, or corporation which provides goods or services to another entity under terms specified in a contract or within a verbal agreement. Unlike an employee, an _____ does not work regularly for an employer but works as and when required, during which time she or he may be subject to the Law of Agency. _____s are usually paid on a freelance basis.

a. Equal Pay Act of 1963
b. Occupational Safety and Health Act
c. Employment protection legislation
d. Independent contractor

Chapter 7. Labor and Employment Laws Applicable to Organized Delivery Systems

45. The _____ of 1952 restricted immigration into the U.S. and is codified under Title 8 of the United States Code. The Act governs primarily immigration and citizenship in the United States. Currently under this act effective from December 24, 1952 to present, the definition of the 'United States' for nationality purposes, was expanded to add Guam; and, effective November 3, 1986, the Commonwealth of the Northern Mariana Islands
   a. Affiliation
   b. Abraham Harold Maslow
   c. Immigration and Nationality Act
   d. Adam Smith

46. In 1975 the United States Supreme Court, in the case of NLRB v. J. Weingarten, Inc., 420 U.S. 251 (1975), upheld a NLRB decision that employees have a right to union representation at investigatory interviews. These rights have become known as the _____.
   a. Negligence
   b. Blue sky law
   c. Railway Labor Act
   d. Weingarten rights

47. The _____ of 1990 (ADA) is the short title of United States (Pub.L. 101-336, 104 Stat. 327, enacted July 26, 1990), codified at 42 U.S.C. Â§ 12101 et seq. It was signed into law on July 26, 1990, by President George H. W. Bush, and later amended with changes effective January 1, 2009. The ADA is a wide-ranging civil rights law that prohibits, under certain circumstances, discrimination based on disability. It affords similar protections against discrimination to Americans with disabilities as the Civil Rights Act of 1964,
   a. Americans with Disabilities Act
   b. Employment discrimination
   c. Australian labour law
   d. Equal Pay Act of 1963

48. The _____ 1970 is an Act of the United Kingdom Parliament which prohibits any less favourable treatment between men and women in terms of pay and conditions of employment. It came into force on 29 December 1975. The term pay is interpreted in a broad sense to include, on top of wages, things like holidays, pension rights, company perks and some kinds of bonuses.
   a. Australian labour law
   b. Oncale v. Sundowner Offshore Services
   c. Architectural Barriers Act of 1968
   d. Equal Pay Act

49. The U.S. _____ of 1973 prohibits discrimination on the basis of disability in programs conducted by Federal agencies, in programs receiving Federal financial assistance, in Federal employment, and in the employment practices of Federal contractors. The standards for determining employment discrimination under the _____ are the same as those used in title I of the Americans with Disabilities Act.

There are four key sections of the Act.

   a. 28-hour day
   b. Rehabilitation Act
   c. 1990 Clean Air Act
   d. 33 Strategies of War

Chapter 8. The Management of Nursing Services

1. _____ is an advertisement in which a particular product specifically mentions a competitor by name for the express purpose of showing why the competitor is inferior to the product naming it.

This should not be confused with parody advertisements, where a fictional product is being advertised for the purpose of poking fun at the particular advertisement, nor should it be confused with the use of a coined brand name for the purpose of comparing the product without actually naming an actual competitor. ('Wikipedia tastes better and is less filling than the Encyclopedia Galactica.')

In the 1980s, during what has been referred to as the cola wars, soft-drink manufacturer Pepsi ran a series of advertisements where people, caught on hidden camera, in a blind taste test, chose Pepsi over rival Coca-Cola.

  a. Comparative advertising
  b. 28-hour day
  c. 33 Strategies of War
  d. 1990 Clean Air Act

2. _____ refers to the movement of cash into or out of a business or financial product. It is usually measured during a specified, finite period of time. Measurement of _____ can be used

   - to determine a project's rate of return or value. The time of _____s into and out of projects are used as inputs in financial models such as internal rate of return, and net present value.
   - to determine problems with a business's liquidity. Being profitable does not necessarily mean being liquid. A company can fail because of a shortage of cash, even while profitable.
   - as an alternate measure of a business's profits when it is believed that accrual accounting concepts do not represent economic realities. For example, a company may be notionally profitable but generating little operational cash (as may be the case for a company that barters its products rather than selling for cash.) In such a case, the company may be deriving additional operating cash by issuing shares evaluating default risk, re-investment requirements, etc.

_____ is a generic term used differently depending on the context. It may be defined by users for their own purposes.

  a. Gross profit
  b. Cash flow
  c. Sweat equity
  d. Gross profit margin

3. _____ is an interdisciplinary field of science and the study of the nature of complex systems in nature, society, and science. More specifically, it is a framework by which one can analyze and/or describe any group of objects that work in concert to produce some result. This could be a single organism, any organization or society, or any electro-mechanical or informational artifact.
  a. Systems thinking
  b. 1990 Clean Air Act
  c. 28-hour day
  d. Systems theory

4. A _____ is a list of the general tasks and responsibilities of a position. Typically, it also includes to whom the position reports, specifications such as the qualifications needed by the person in the job, salary range for the position, etc. A _____ is usually developed by conducting a job analysis, which includes examining the tasks and sequences of tasks necessary to perform the job.
  a. Recruitment Process Insourcing
  b. Job description
  c. Recruitment
  d. Recruitment advertising

Chapter 8. The Management of Nursing Services

5. _____ of the learning curve effect and the closely related experience curve effect express the relationship between equations for experience and efficiency or between efficiency gains and investment in the effort. The experience of 'learning curves' was first observed by the 19th Century German psychologist Hermann Ebbinghaus according to the difficulty of memorizing varying numbers of verbal stimuli, and subsequent learning about the complex processes of learning are discussed in the

.

The rule used for representing the learning curve effect states that the more times a task has been performed, the less time will be required on each subsequent iteration.

- a. Distribution
- b. Spatial Decision Support Systems
- c. Point biserial correlation coefficient
- d. Models

6. In microeconomics and management, the term _____ describes a style of management control. Vertically integrated companies are united through a hierarchy with a common owner. Usually each member of the hierarchy produces a different product or (market-specific) service, and the products combine to satisfy a common need.
   - a. 33 Strategies of War
   - b. 28-hour day
   - c. 1990 Clean Air Act
   - d. Vertical integration

7. In microeconomics and strategic management, the term _____ describes a type of ownership and control. It is a strategy used by a business or corporation that seeks to sell a type of product in numerous markets. _____ in marketing is much more common than vertical integration is in production.
   - a. Farmshoring
   - b. Horizontal integration
   - c. Career development
   - d. No-bid contract

8. In probability theory, a probability distribution is called _____ if its cumulative distribution function is _____. This is equivalent to saying that for random variables X with the distribution in question, Pr[X = a] = 0 for all real numbers a, i.e.: the probability that X attains the value a is zero, for any number a. If the distribution of X is _____ then X is called a _____ random variable.
   - a. Decision tree pruning
   - b. Pay Band
   - c. Connectionist expert systems
   - d. Continuous

9. Quality management can be considered to have three main components: quality control, quality assurance and _____. Quality management is focused not only on product quality, but also the means to achieve it. Quality management therefore uses quality assurance and control of processes as well as products to achieve more consistent quality.
   - a. 1990 Clean Air Act
   - b. Quality management
   - c. 28-hour day
   - d. Quality improvement

Chapter 9. Planning Healthcare Facilities and Managing the Development Process

1. A chief executive officer (_____) or chief executive is one of the highest-ranking corporate officer (executive) or administrator in charge of total management. An individual selected as President and _____ of a corporation, company, organization, or agency, reports to the board of directors. In internal communication and press releases, many companies capitalize the term and those of other high positions, even when they are not proper nouns.
    a. Director of communications
    b. Portfolio manager
    c. CEO
    d. Chief executive officer

2. _____ is an advertisement in which a particular product specifically mentions a competitor by name for the express purpose of showing why the competitor is inferior to the product naming it.

   This should not be confused with parody advertisements, where a fictional product is being advertised for the purpose of poking fun at the particular advertisement, nor should it be confused with the use of a coined brand name for the purpose of comparing the product without actually naming an actual competitor. ('Wikipedia tastes better and is less filling than the Encyclopedia Galactica.')

   In the 1980s, during what has been referred to as the cola wars, soft-drink manufacturer Pepsi ran a series of advertisements where people, caught on hidden camera, in a blind taste test, chose Pepsi over rival Coca-Cola.

    a. 1990 Clean Air Act
    b. 28-hour day
    c. 33 Strategies of War
    d. Comparative advertising

3. _____, in microeconomics, are the cost advantages that a business obtains due to expansion. They are factors that cause a producer's average cost per unit to fall as scale is increased. _____ is a long run concept and refers to reductions in unit cost as the size of a facility, or scale, increases.
    a. A Stake in the Outcome
    b. A4e
    c. Economies of scale
    d. Economies of scope

4. The term '_____' refers to the concept of collecting information and attempting to spot a pattern in the information. In some fields of study, the term '_____' has more formally-defined meanings.

   In project management _____ is a mathematical technique that uses historical results to predict future outcome.

    a. Least squares
    b. Regression analysis
    c. Stepwise regression
    d. Trend analysis

5. _____ is subcontracting a process, such as product design or manufacturing, to a third-party company. The decision to outsource is often made in the interest of lowering cost or making better use of time and energy costs, redirecting or conserving energy directed at the competencies of a particular business, or to make more efficient use of land, labor, capital, (information) technology and resources. _____ became part of the business lexicon during the 1980s.
    a. Opinion leadership
    b. Unemployment insurance
    c. Outsourcing
    d. Operant conditioning

6. A _____ or chief executive is one of the highest-ranking corporate officer (executive) or administrator in charge of total management. An individual selected as President and _____ of a corporation, company, organization, or agency, reports to the board of directors. In internal communication and press releases, many companies capitalize the term and those of other high positions, even when they are not proper nouns.

Chapter 9. Planning Healthcare Facilities and Managing the Development Process

a. Purchasing manager
c. Chief brand officer
b. Financial analyst
d. Chief executive officer

7. While _____ literally refers to a person responsible for the performance of duties involved in running an organization, the exact meaning of the role is variable, depending on the organization.

While there is no clear line between executive or principal and inferior officers, principal officers are high-level officials in the executive branch of U.S. government such as department heads of independent agencies. In Humphrey's Executor v. United States, 295 U.S. 602 (1935), the Court distinguished between _____s and quasi-legislative or quasi-judicial officers by stating that the former serve at the pleasure of the President and may be removed at his discretion.

a. Australian Fair Pay and Conditions Standard
c. Easement
b. Unreported employment
d. Executive officer

8. _____ refers to the movement of cash into or out of a business or financial product. It is usually measured during a specified, finite period of time. Measurement of _____ can be used

- to determine a project's rate of return or value. The time of _____s into and out of projects are used as inputs in financial models such as internal rate of return, and net present value.
- to determine problems with a business's liquidity. Being profitable does not necessarily mean being liquid. A company can fail because of a shortage of cash, even while profitable.
- as an alternate measure of a business's profits when it is believed that accrual accounting concepts do not represent economic realities. For example, a company may be notionally profitable but generating little operational cash (as may be the case for a company that barters its products rather than selling for cash.) In such a case, the company may be deriving additional operating cash by issuing shares evaluating default risk, re-investment requirements, etc.

_____ is a generic term used differently depending on the context. It may be defined by users for their own purposes.

a. Gross profit margin
c. Gross profit
b. Sweat equity
d. Cash flow

9. _____ is the discipline of planning, organizing and managing resources to bring about the successful completion of specific project goals and objectives. It is often closely related to and sometimes conflated with Program management.

A project is a finite endeavor--having specific start and completion dates--undertaken to meet particular goals and objectives, usually to bring about beneficial change or added value.

a. Project engineer
c. Precedence diagram
b. Project management
d. Work package

10. A _____ is a professional who provides advice in a particular area of expertise such as management, accountancy, the environment, entertainment, technology, law , human resources, marketing, medicine, finance, economics, public affairs, communication, engineering, sound system design, graphic design, or waste management.

Chapter 9. Planning Healthcare Facilities and Managing the Development Process

A _____ is usually an expert or a professional in a specific field and has a wide knowledge of the subject matter. A _____ usually works for a consultancy firm or is self-employed, and engages with multiple and changing clients.

a. 1990 Clean Air Act
b. 33 Strategies of War
c. Consultant
d. 28-hour day

11. _____ is a civil designation for persons who are incorporated in a fixed or permanent way to a society or group: regular member of the working staff, permanent staff distinguished from a supernumerary.

The term '_____' and its counterpart, 'supernumerary,' originated in Spanish and Latin American academy and government; it is now also used in countries all over the world, such as France, the U.S., England, Italy, etc.

There are _____ members of surgical organizations, of universities, of gastronomical associations, etc.

a. Abraham Harold Maslow
b. Numerary
c. Adam Smith
d. Affiliation

12. _____ refers either to the study and practice of the managerial and technological aspects of the construction industry (including construction, construction science, _____, and construction technology) or to a business model where one party to a construction contract serves as a construction consultant providing both design and construction advice.

The _____ Association of America says the 120 most common responsibilities of a Construction Manager fall into the following 7 categories: Project Management Planning, Cost Management, Time Management, Quality Management, Contract Administration, Safety Management, and _____ Professional Practice which includes specific activities like defining the responsibilities and management structure of the project management team, organizing and leading by implementing project controls, defining roles and responsibilities and developing communication protocols, and identifying elements of project design and construction likely to give rise to disputes and claims.

a. 33 Strategies of War
b. Construction Management
c. 1990 Clean Air Act
d. 28-hour day

Chapter 10. Financing of Healthcare Facilities

1. A _____ or chief executive is one of the highest-ranking corporate officer (executive) or administrator in charge of total management. An individual selected as President and _____ of a corporation, company, organization, or agency, reports to the board of directors. In internal communication and press releases, many companies capitalize the term and those of other high positions, even when they are not proper nouns.
   a. Financial analyst
   b. Chief brand officer
   c. Purchasing manager
   d. Chief executive officer

2. The _____ of a company or public agency is the corporate officer primarily responsible for managing the financial risks of the business or agency. This officer is also responsible for financial planning and record-keeping, as well as financial reporting to higher management. (In recent years, however, the role has expanded to encompass communicating financial performance and forecasts to the analyst community.)
   a. Chief financial officer
   b. 33 Strategies of War
   c. 28-hour day
   d. 1990 Clean Air Act

3. While _____ literally refers to a person responsible for the performance of duties involved in running an organization, the exact meaning of the role is variable, depending on the organization.

   While there is no clear line between executive or principal and inferior officers, principal officers are high-level officials in the executive branch of U.S. government such as department heads of independent agencies. In Humphrey's Executor v. United States, 295 U.S. 602 (1935), the Court distinguished between _____s and quasi-legislative or quasi-judicial officers by stating that the former serve at the pleasure of the President and may be removed at his discretion.

   a. Easement
   b. Unreported employment
   c. Australian Fair Pay and Conditions Standard
   d. Executive officer

4. In economics, _____ is the desire to own something and the ability to pay for it. The term _____ signifies the ability or the willingness to buy a particular commodity at a given point of time.
   a. 1990 Clean Air Act
   b. 28-hour day
   c. 33 Strategies of War
   d. Demand

5. In business and accounting, _____s are everything of value that is owned by a person or company. Any property or object of value that one possesses, usually considered as applicable to the payment of one's debts is considered an _____. Simplistically stated, _____s are things of value that can be readily converted into cash.
   a. A Stake in the Outcome
   b. AAAI
   c. A4e
   d. Asset

6. Title _____s serve as guarantees to the recipient of property, ensuring that the recipient receives what he or she bargained for. The English _____s of title, sometimes included in deeds to real property, are that the grantor is lawfully seized (in fee simple) of the property, (2) that the grantor has the right to convey the property to the grantee, (3) that the property is conveyed without encumbrances (this _____ is frequently modified to allow for certain encumbrances), (4) that the grantor has done no act to encumber the property, (5) that the grantee shall have quiet possession of the property, and (6) that the grantor will execute such further assurances of the land as may be requisite (Nos. 3 and 4, which overlap significantly, are sometimes treated as one item.)
   a. Hostile work environment
   b. Business valuation
   c. Trade secret
   d. Covenant

Chapter 10. Financing of Healthcare Facilities

7. Market _____ is a business, economics or investment term that refers to an asset's ability to be easily converted through an act of buying or selling without causing a significant movement in the price and with minimum loss of value. Money, or cash on hand, is the most liquid asset. An act of exchange of a less liquid asset with a more liquid asset is called liquidation.
   a. 28-hour day
   b. 1990 Clean Air Act
   c. 33 Strategies of War
   d. Liquidity

8. _____ plant, and equipment, is a term used in accountancy for assets and property which cannot easily be converted into cash. This can be compared with current assets such as cash or bank accounts, which are described as liquid assets. In most cases, only tangible assets are referred to as fixed.
   a. 1990 Clean Air Act
   b. Fixed asset
   c. 33 Strategies of War
   d. 28-hour day

9. A _____ is an entity formed between two or more parties to undertake economic activity together. The parties agree to create a new entity by both contributing equity, and they then share in the revenues, expenses, and control of the enterprise. The venture can be for one specific project only, or a continuing business relationship such as the Fuji Xerox _____.
   a. Meritor Savings Bank v. Vinson
   b. Patent
   c. Joint venture
   d. Civil Rights Act of 1991

10. A _____ is a type of business entity in which partners (owners) share with each other the profits or losses of the business. _____s are often favored over corporations for taxation purposes, as the _____ structure does not generally incur a tax on profits before it is distributed to the partners (i.e. there is no dividend tax levied.) However, depending on the _____ structure and the jurisdiction in which it operates, owners of a _____ may be exposed to greater personal liability than they would as shareholders of a corporation.
    a. Federal Employers Liability Act
    b. Mediation
    c. Due process
    d. Partnership

11. _____ is an advertisement in which a particular product specifically mentions a competitor by name for the express purpose of showing why the competitor is inferior to the product naming it.

This should not be confused with parody advertisements, where a fictional product is being advertised for the purpose of poking fun at the particular advertisement, nor should it be confused with the use of a coined brand name for the purpose of comparing the product without actually naming an actual competitor. ('Wikipedia tastes better and is less filling than the Encyclopedia Galactica.')

In the 1980s, during what has been referred to as the cola wars, soft-drink manufacturer Pepsi ran a series of advertisements where people, caught on hidden camera, in a blind taste test, chose Pepsi over rival Coca-Cola.

   a. 33 Strategies of War
   b. 28-hour day
   c. 1990 Clean Air Act
   d. Comparative advertising

12. An _____ is a person who has possession of an enterprise and assumes significant accountability for the inherent risks and the outcome. It is an ambitious leader who combines land, labor, and capital to create and market new goods or services. The term is a loanword from French and was first defined by the Irish economist Richard Cantillon.

Chapter 10. Financing of Healthcare Facilities 61

a. Entrepreneur
c. A Stake in the Outcome
b. A4e
d. AAAI

13. A _____ is a form of partnership similar to a general partnership, except that in addition to one or more general partners (GPs), there are one or more limited partners (_____s.) It is a partnership in which only one partner is required to be a general partner.

The GPs are, in all major respects, in the same legal position as partners in a conventional firm, i.e. they have management control, share the right to use partnership property, share the profits of the firm in predefined proportions, and have joint and several liability for the debts of the partnership.

a. Limited Partnership
c. Growth capital
b. Private equity
d. Pension fund

14. The _____ , which includes its 1976 revision called the Revised _____, is a uniform act (similar to a model statute), proposed by the National Conference of Commissioners on Uniform State Laws ('NCCUSL') for the governance of business partnerships by U.S. States. The NCCUSL promulgated the original _____ in 1916 and the most recent revision in 2001.

The NCCUSL promulgated the original _____ in 1916, which is now called the _____ (1916) or _____ (1916); a 1976 revision named the Revised _____ which is also now called the _____ (1976), _____ (1976) or RUniform Limited Partnership Act (1976); a 1985 revision named _____ (1976) with 1985 Amendments, which is also now called _____ (1985) or RUniform Limited Partnership Act (1985); and a 2001 revision that was colloquially called Re-RUniform Limited Partnership Act during the drafting process but then was officially named the _____ (2001) or _____ (2001.)

a. A Stake in the Outcome
c. Uniform Limited Partnership Act
b. AAAI
d. A4e

15. _____ is the state or fact of exclusive rights and control over property, which may be an object, land/real estate or intellectual property. An _____ right is also referred to as title. The concept of _____ has existed for thousands of years and in all cultures.
a. A4e
c. A Stake in the Outcome
b. Emanation of the state
d. Ownership

16. _____ is a concept whereby a person's financial liability is limited to a fixed sum, most commonly the value of a person's investment in a company or partnership with _____. In other words, if a company with _____ is sued, then the plaintiffs are suing the company, not its owners or investors. A shareholder in a limited company is not personally liable for any of the debts of the company, other than for the value of his investment in that company.
a. Toxic Substances Control Act
c. Limited liability
b. Partnership
d. Privity

Chapter 10. Financing of Healthcare Facilities

17. A limited liability company in the law of the vast majority of United States jurisdictions is a legal form of business company that provides limited liability to its owners. Often incorrectly called a '_____' (instead of company), it is a hybrid business entity having certain characteristics of both a corporation and a partnership or sole proprietorship (depending on how many owners there are.) The primary characteristic an _____ shares with a corporation is limited liability, and the primary characteristic it shares with a partnership is the availability of pass-through income taxation.
   a. Growth capital
   b. Limited liability corporation
   c. Seed round
   d. Management buyout

18. _____ refers to the movement of cash into or out of a business or financial product. It is usually measured during a specified, finite period of time. Measurement of _____ can be used

   - to determine a project's rate of return or value. The time of _____s into and out of projects are used as inputs in financial models such as internal rate of return, and net present value.
   - to determine problems with a business's liquidity. Being profitable does not necessarily mean being liquid. A company can fail because of a shortage of cash, even while profitable.
   - as an alternate measure of a business's profits when it is believed that accrual accounting concepts do not represent economic realities. For example, a company may be notionally profitable but generating little operational cash (as may be the case for a company that barters its products rather than selling for cash.) In such a case, the company may be deriving additional operating cash by issuing shares evaluating default risk, re-investment requirements, etc.

   _____ is a generic term used differently depending on the context. It may be defined by users for their own purposes.

   a. Sweat equity
   b. Gross profit
   c. Cash flow
   d. Gross profit margin

19. A _____ is a state law in the United States that regulates the offering and sale of securities to protect the public from fraud. Though the specific provisions of these laws vary among states, they all require the registration of all securities offerings and sales, as well as of stock brokers and brokerage firms. Each state's _____ is administered by its appropriate regulatory agency, and most also provide private causes of action for private investors who have been injured by securities fraud.
   a. Civil Rights Act of 1875
   b. Hostile work environment
   c. Blue sky law
   d. Duty of loyalty

20. The U.S. _____ is an independent agency of the United States government which holds primary responsibility for enforcing the federal securities laws and regulating the securities industry, the nation's stock and options exchanges, and other electronic securities markets. The SEC was created by section 4 of the Securities Exchange Act of 1934 (now codified as 15 U.S.C. § 78d and commonly referred to as the 1934 Act.)
   a. 33 Strategies of War
   b. 28-hour day
   c. 1990 Clean Air Act
   d. Securities and Exchange Commission

21. A _____ is a funding round of securities which are sold without a initial public offering, usually to a small number of chosen private investors. In the United States, these placements are not subject to the Securities Act of 1933 and do not have to be registered with the Securities and Exchange Commission, although the sale must conform to SEC rules. _____s may typically consist of stocks, shares or warrants and purchasers are often institutional investors such as banks, insurance companies or pension funds.

a. Labor intensive
c. Niche market
b. Choquet integral
d. Private placement

22. _____ , also referred to simply as a 'public offering' or 'flotation,' is when a company issues common stock or shares to the public for the first time. They are often issued by smaller, younger companies seeking capital to expand, but can also be done by large privately-owned companies looking to become publicly traded.

In an _____ the issuer may obtain the assistance of an underwriting firm, which helps it determine what type of security to issue (common or preferred), best offering price and time to bring it to market.

a. Outsourcing
c. Occupational Safety and Health Administration
b. Unemployment insurance
d. Initial public offering

Chapter 11. Marketing Healthcare Services

1. _____ is an integrated communications-based process through which individuals and communities discover that existing and newly-identified needs and wants may be satisfied by the products and services of others.

_____ is defined by the American _____ Association as the activity, set of institutions, and processes for creating, communicating, delivering, and exchanging offerings that have value for customers, clients, partners, and society at large. The term developed from the original meaning which referred literally to going to market, as in shopping, or going to a market to buy or sell goods or services.

    a. Disruptive technology
    b. Customer relationship management
    c. Market development
    d. Marketing

2. The _____ is generally accepted as the use and specification of the 'four P's' describing the strategic position of a product in the marketplace. One version of the _____ originated in 1948 when James Culliton said that a marketing decision should be a result of something similar to a recipe. This version was used in 1953 when Neil Borden, in his American Marketing Association presidential address, took the recipe idea one step further and coined the term 'marketing-mix'.

    a. Marketing mix
    b. 28-hour day
    c. 1990 Clean Air Act
    d. 33 Strategies of War

3. A _____ is a type of business entity in which partners (owners) share with each other the profits or losses of the business. _____s are often favored over corporations for taxation purposes, as the _____ structure does not generally incur a tax on profits before it is distributed to the partners (i.e. there is no dividend tax levied.) However, depending on the _____ structure and the jurisdiction in which it operates, owners of a _____ may be exposed to greater personal liability than they would as shareholders of a corporation.

    a. Partnership
    b. Due process
    c. Mediation
    d. Federal Employers Liability Act

4. In microeconomics and management, the term _____ describes a style of management control. Vertically integrated companies are united through a hierarchy with a common owner. Usually each member of the hierarchy produces a different product or (market-specific) service, and the products combine to satisfy a common need.

    a. 33 Strategies of War
    b. 1990 Clean Air Act
    c. 28-hour day
    d. Vertical integration

5. _____ describes commerce transactions between businesses, such as between a manufacturer and a wholesaler, or between a wholesaler and a retailer. Contrasting terms are business-to-consumer (B2C) and business-to-government (B2G.)

The volume of B2B transactions is much higher than the volume of B2C transactions.

    a. Category management
    b. Product bundling
    c. Market environment
    d. Business-to-business

6. A _____ is a form of qualitative research in which a group of people are asked about their attitude towards a product, service, concept, advertisement, idea, or packaging. Questions are asked in an interactive group setting where participants are free to talk with other group members.

Chapter 11. Marketing Healthcare Services

The first _____s were created at the Bureau of Applied Social Research by associate director, sociologist Robert K. Merton.

a. Marketing research
b. Market analysis
c. 1990 Clean Air Act
d. Focus group

7. _____ is a form of communication that typically attempts to persuade potential customers to purchase or to consume more of a particular brand of product or service. 'While now central to the contemporary global economy and the reproduction of global production networks, it is only quite recently that _____ has been more than a marginal influence on patterns of sales and production. The formation of modern _____ was intimately bound up with the emergence of new forms of monopoly capitalism around the end of the 19th and beginning of the 20th century as one element in corporate strategies to create, organize and where possible control markets, especially for mass produced consumer goods.

a. A4e
b. A Stake in the Outcome
c. AAAI
d. Advertising

8. In economics, _____ is the desire to own something and the ability to pay for it. The term _____ signifies the ability or the willingness to buy a particular commodity at a given point of time.

a. 1990 Clean Air Act
b. 28-hour day
c. 33 Strategies of War
d. Demand

9. _____ advertising (DTC advertising) usually refers to the marketing of pharmaceutical products but can apply in other areas as well. This form of advertising is directed toward patients, rather than healthcare professionals. Forms of DTC advertising include TV, print, radio and other mass and social media.

a. Direct-to-consumer
b. 28-hour day
c. 33 Strategies of War
d. 1990 Clean Air Act

10. _____ refers to planned and systematic production processes that provide confidence in a product's suitability for its intended purpose. Refer to the definition by Merriam-Webster for further information. It is a set of activities intended to ensure that products (goods and/or services) satisfy customer requirements in a systematic, reliable fashion.

a. Risk assessment
b. Quality Assurance
c. 28-hour day
d. 1990 Clean Air Act

11. _____ is a broad label that refers to any individuals or households that use goods and services generated within the economy. The concept of a _____ is used in different contexts, so that the usage and significance of the term may vary.

Typically when business people and economists talk of _____s they are talking about person as _____, an aggregated commodity item with little individuality other than that expressed in the buy/not-buy decision.

a. 1990 Clean Air Act
b. 28-hour day
c. 33 Strategies of War
d. Consumer

12. _____ is one of the four Ps of the marketing mix. The other three aspects are product, promotion, and place. It is also a key variable in microeconomic price allocation theory.

a. Penetration pricing
b. Pricing
c. Price floor
d. Transfer pricing

13. _____ is the activity that the selling organization undertakes to reduce customer account defections. The success of this activity is when the customer account places an additional order before a 12-month period has expired. Note that ideally these orders will need to contribute similar financial amounts to the previous 12 months.

a. Foreign ownership
b. Business rule
c. Customer retention
d. Process automation

14. A _____ is a government- or group-imposed limit on how low a price can be charged for a product. In order for a _____ to be effective, it must be greater than the equilibrium price. An ineffective _____, below equilibrium price.

A _____ can be set below the free-market equilibrium price.

a. Price floor
b. Pricing objectives
c. Transfer pricing
d. Penetration pricing

15. _____ consists of the mental process of thinking involved with the process of judging the merits of multiple options and selecting one of them for action. Some simple examples include deciding whether to get up in the morning or go back to sleep, or selecting a given route for a journey. More complex examples (often decisions that affect what a person thinks or their core beliefs) include choosing a lifestyle, religious affiliation, or political position.

a. Groups decision making
b. Trade study
c. Choice
d. Championship mobilization

16. _____ is the provision of service to customers before, during and after a purchase.

According to Turban et al. (2002), '_____ is a series of activities designed to enhance the level of customer satisfaction - that is, the feeling that a product or service has met the customer expectation.'

Its importance varies by product, industry and customer; defective or broken merchandise can be exchanged, often only with a receipt and within a specified time frame.

a. Service rate
b. 1990 Clean Air Act
c. 28-hour day
d. Customer service

17. _____ is an advertisement in which a particular product specifically mentions a competitor by name for the express purpose of showing why the competitor is inferior to the product naming it.

This should not be confused with parody advertisements, where a fictional product is being advertised for the purpose of poking fun at the particular advertisement, nor should it be confused with the use of a coined brand name for the purpose of comparing the product without actually naming an actual competitor. ('Wikipedia tastes better and is less filling than the Encyclopedia Galactica.')

In the 1980s, during what has been referred to as the cola wars, soft-drink manufacturer Pepsi ran a series of advertisements where people, caught on hidden camera, in a blind taste test, chose Pepsi over rival Coca-Cola.

a. 33 Strategies of War	b. 28-hour day
c. 1990 Clean Air Act	d. Comparative advertising

18. _____, a business term, is a measure of how products and services supplied by a company meet or surpass customer expectation. It is seen as a key performance indicator within business and is part of the four perspectives of a Balanced Scorecard.

In a competitive marketplace where businesses compete for customers, _____ is seen as a key differentiator and increasingly has become a key element of business strategy.

a. Customer satisfaction	b. Horizontal integration
c. Critical Success Factor	d. Foreign ownership

Chapter 12. Health Care Information Systems: An Organized Delivery System Perspective

1. _____ is an advertisement in which a particular product specifically mentions a competitor by name for the express purpose of showing why the competitor is inferior to the product naming it.

This should not be confused with parody advertisements, where a fictional product is being advertised for the purpose of poking fun at the particular advertisement, nor should it be confused with the use of a coined brand name for the purpose of comparing the product without actually naming an actual competitor. ('Wikipedia tastes better and is less filling than the Encyclopedia Galactica.')

In the 1980s, during what has been referred to as the cola wars, soft-drink manufacturer Pepsi ran a series of advertisements where people, caught on hidden camera, in a blind taste test, chose Pepsi over rival Coca-Cola.

a. 28-hour day
b. Comparative advertising
c. 33 Strategies of War
d. 1990 Clean Air Act

2. The term '_____' refers to the concept of collecting information and attempting to spot a pattern in the information. In some fields of study, the term '_____' has more formally-defined meanings.

In project management _____ is a mathematical technique that uses historical results to predict future outcome.

a. Least squares
b. Regression analysis
c. Stepwise regression
d. Trend analysis

3. _____ is the incidence or process of transferring ownership of a business, enterprise, agency or public service from the public sector (government) to the private sector (business.) In a broader sense, _____ refers to transfer of any government function to the private sector including governmental functions like revenue collection and law enforcement.

a. 28-hour day
b. Performance reports
c. 1990 Clean Air Act
d. Privatization

4. _____ refers to the movement of cash into or out of a business or financial product. It is usually measured during a specified, finite period of time. Measurement of _____ can be used

- to determine a project's rate of return or value. The time of _____s into and out of projects are used as inputs in financial models such as internal rate of return, and net present value.
- to determine problems with a business's liquidity. Being profitable does not necessarily mean being liquid. A company can fail because of a shortage of cash, even while profitable.
- as an alternate measure of a business's profits when it is believed that accrual accounting concepts do not represent economic realities. For example, a company may be notionally profitable but generating little operational cash (as may be the case for a company that barters its products rather than selling for cash.) In such a case, the company may be deriving additional operating cash by issuing shares evaluating default risk, re-investment requirements, etc.

_____ is a generic term used differently depending on the context. It may be defined by users for their own purposes.

a. Sweat equity
b. Gross profit margin
c. Gross profit
d. Cash flow

Chapter 12. Health Care Information Systems: An Organized Delivery System Perspective 69

5. _____ are a class of electronic meeting systems, a collaboration technology designed to support meetings and group work . _____ are distinct from computer supported cooperative work (CSCW) technologies as _____ are more focused on task support, whereas CSCW tools provide general communication support .

_____ were referred to as a Group Support System (GSS) or an electronic meeting system since they shared similar foundations.

a. Hoshin Kanri
b. Learning organization
c. Group decision support systems
d. 1990 Clean Air Act

6. _____ constitute a class of computer-based information systems including knowledge-based systems that support decision-making activities.

_____ are a specific class of computerized information systems that supports business and organizational decision-making activities. A properly-designed _____ is an interactive software-based system intended to help decision makers compile useful information from raw data, documents, personal knowledge, and/or business models to identify and solve problems and make decisions.

a. Decision support systems
b. 1990 Clean Air Act
c. 28-hour day
d. Spatial Decision Support Systems

7. An _____ is a private computer network that uses Internet technologies to securely share any part of an organization's information or operational systems with its employees. Sometimes the term refers only to the organization's internal website, but often it is a more extensive part of the organization's computer infrastructure and private websites are an important component and focal point of internal communication and collaboration.

An _____ is built from the same concepts and technologies used for the Internet, such as client-server computing and the Internet Protocol Suite (TCP/IP.)

a. AAAI
b. A Stake in the Outcome
c. Intranet
d. A4e

8. A _____ is a concept used in strategic management that groups companies within an industry that have similar business models or similar combinations of strategies. For example, the restaurant industry can be divided into several _____s including fast-food and fine-dining based on variables such as preparation time, pricing, and presentation. The number of groups within an industry and their composition depends on the dimensions used to define the groups.

a. Strategic group
b. Strategic drift
c. Corporate strategy
d. Strategic business unit

Chapter 13. Management Engineering

1. Industrial engineering is also known as operations management, management science, systems engineering, or manufacturing engineering; a distinction that seems to depend on the viewpoint or motives of the user. Recruiters or educational establishments use the names to differentiate themselves from others. In healthcare, for example, _____ are more commonly known as management engineers or health systems engineers.
   a. A Stake in the Outcome
   b. A4e
   c. AAAI
   d. Industrial Engineers

2. _____ or health systems engineering is a type of engineering in the field of healthcare.

Health system engineering includes many different disciplines such as industrial engineering, operations research, management science and quality management.

   a. 28-hour day
   b. 33 Strategies of War
   c. 1990 Clean Air Act
   d. Management engineering

3. _____ is also known as operations management, management science, systems engineering, or manufacturing engineering; a distinction that seems to depend on the viewpoint or motives of the user. Recruiters or educational establishments use the names to differentiate themselves from others. In healthcare, for example, industrial engineers are more commonly known as management engineers or health systems engineers.
   a. AAAI
   b. A Stake in the Outcome
   c. A4e
   d. Industrial Engineering

4. In economics, business, retail, and accounting, a _____ is the value of money that has been used up to produce something, and hence is not available for use anymore. In economics, a _____ is an alternative that is given up as a result of a decision. In business, the _____ may be one of acquisition, in which case the amount of money expended to acquire it is counted as _____.
   a. Cost overrun
   b. Fixed costs
   c. Cost allocation
   d. Cost

5. _____ is an organization's process of defining its strategy and making decisions on allocating its resources to pursue this strategy, including its capital and people. Various business analysis techniques can be used in _____, including SWOT analysis (Strengths, Weaknesses, Opportunities, and Threats) and PEST analysis (Political, Economic, Social, and Technological analysis) or STEER analysis involving Socio-cultural, Technological, Economic, Ecological, and Regulatory factors and EPISTEL (Environment, Political, Informatic, Social, Technological, Economic and Legal)

_____ is the formal consideration of an organization's future course. All _____ deals with at least one of three key questions:

   1. 'What do we do?'
   2. 'For whom do we do it?'
   3. 'How do we excel?'

In business _____, the third question is better phrased 'How can we beat or avoid competition?'. (Bradford and Duncan, page 1.)

a. 28-hour day
b. 33 Strategies of War
c. 1990 Clean Air Act
d. Strategic planning

6. A _____ is a list of the general tasks and responsibilities of a position. Typically, it also includes to whom the position reports, specifications such as the qualifications needed by the person in the job, salary range for the position, etc. A _____ is usually developed by conducting a job analysis, which includes examining the tasks and sequences of tasks necessary to perform the job.
   a. Recruitment Process Insourcing
   b. Recruitment
   c. Recruitment advertising
   d. Job description

7. _____ refers to metrics and measures of output from production processes, per unit of input. Labor _____, for example, is typically measured as a ratio of output per labor-hour, an input. _____ may be conceived of as a metrics of the technical or engineering efficiency of production.
   a. Master production schedule
   b. Productivity
   c. Remanufacturing
   d. Value engineering

8. The maturity road mapping method (MRMM) is a general procedure to increase the speed and reduce the cost of achieving the maturity condition in a process, product or an organization and with similar approach like PDCA and we call it as _____.

This methodology was developed from 1985 and completed during more than two decades. The basic elements of this model are three as follows; 1- software 2- hardware 3- roadware

Book over of MRM Components of economic growth through productivity (Saari 2006)

The logical manner of this approach is like the periodic table of the chemical elements(by Dmitri Mendeleev) that with defining the trend of electron circulation around cell of the atom helps understanding and predicting unknown atoms.

   a. Deflation
   b. Productivity management
   c. Perfect competition
   d. Gross domestic product

9. _____ is a term that is used to describe a specialized form of management that is required to successfully lead engineering personnel and projects. The average Engineering Manager retires at 50-60 years of age. The term can be used to describe either functional management or project management- leading technical professionals who are working in the fields of product development, manufacturing, construction, design engineering, industrial engineering, technology, production, or any other field that employs personnel who perform an engineering function.
   a. Efficient Consumer Response
   b. Executive development
   c. ISO/TC 223
   d. Engineering management

10. In engineering and manufacturing, _____ and quality engineering are used in developing systems to ensure products or services are designed and produced to meet or exceed customer requirements. Refer to the definition by Merriam-Webster for further information . These systems are often developed in conjunction with other business and engineering disciplines using a cross-functional approach.

a. Quality control
b. Statistical process control
c. Process capability
d. Single Minute Exchange of Die

11. _____ is one of the managerial functions like planning, organizing, staffing and directing. It is an important function because it helps to check the errors and to take the corrective action so that deviation from standards are minimized and stated goals of the organization are achieved in desired manner. According to modern concepts, _____ is a foreseeing action whereas earlier concept of _____ was used only when errors were detected. _____ in management means setting standards, measuring actual performance and taking corrective action.

a. Control
b. Turnover
c. Schedule of reinforcement
d. Decision tree pruning

12. _____ is an advertisement in which a particular product specifically mentions a competitor by name for the express purpose of showing why the competitor is inferior to the product naming it.

This should not be confused with parody advertisements, where a fictional product is being advertised for the purpose of poking fun at the particular advertisement, nor should it be confused with the use of a coined brand name for the purpose of comparing the product without actually naming an actual competitor. ('Wikipedia tastes better and is less filling than the Encyclopedia Galactica.')

In the 1980s, during what has been referred to as the cola wars, soft-drink manufacturer Pepsi ran a series of advertisements where people, caught on hidden camera, in a blind taste test, chose Pepsi over rival Coca-Cola.

a. 1990 Clean Air Act
b. Comparative advertising
c. 33 Strategies of War
d. 28-hour day

13. In neuroscience, the _____ is a collection of brain structures which attempts to regulate and control behavior by inducing pleasurable effects.

A psychological reward is a process that reinforces behavior -- something that, when offered, causes a behavior to increase in intensity. Reward is an operational concept for describing the positive value an individual ascribes to an object, behavioral act or an internal physical state.

a. 33 Strategies of War
b. 1990 Clean Air Act
c. 28-hour day
d. Reward system

14. A chief executive officer (_____) or chief executive is one of the highest-ranking corporate officer (executive) or administrator in charge of total management. An individual selected as President and _____ of a corporation, company, organization, or agency, reports to the board of directors. In internal communication and press releases, many companies capitalize the term and those of other high positions, even when they are not proper nouns.

a. Director of communications
b. Portfolio manager
c. Chief executive officer
d. CEO

15. In queueing theory, _____ is the proportion of the system's resources which is used by the traffic which arrives at it. It should be strictly less than one for the system to function well. It is usually represented by the symbol ρ.

a. Utilization
b. AAAI
c. A Stake in the Outcome
d. A4e

16. _____ is one of the four Ps of the marketing mix. The other three aspects are product, promotion, and place. It is also a key variable in microeconomic price allocation theory.
   a. Transfer pricing
   b. Pricing
   c. Price floor
   d. Penetration pricing

17. _____ consists of the mental process of thinking involved with the process of judging the merits of multiple options and selecting one of them for action. Some simple examples include deciding whether to get up in the morning or go back to sleep, or selecting a given route for a journey. More complex examples (often decisions that affect what a person thinks or their core beliefs) include choosing a lifestyle, religious affiliation, or political position.
   a. Championship mobilization
   b. Groups decision making
   c. Trade study
   d. Choice

18. _____ is a broad label that refers to any individuals or households that use goods and services generated within the economy. The concept of a _____ is used in different contexts, so that the usage and significance of the term may vary.

Typically when business people and economists talk of _____s they are talking about person as _____, an aggregated commodity item with little individuality other than that expressed in the buy/not-buy decision.

   a. 1990 Clean Air Act
   b. 28-hour day
   c. 33 Strategies of War
   d. Consumer

Chapter 14. Ambulatory Care

1. _____ is an advertisement in which a particular product specifically mentions a competitor by name for the express purpose of showing why the competitor is inferior to the product naming it.

This should not be confused with parody advertisements, where a fictional product is being advertised for the purpose of poking fun at the particular advertisement, nor should it be confused with the use of a coined brand name for the purpose of comparing the product without actually naming an actual competitor. ('Wikipedia tastes better and is less filling than the Encyclopedia Galactica.')

In the 1980s, during what has been referred to as the cola wars, soft-drink manufacturer Pepsi ran a series of advertisements where people, caught on hidden camera, in a blind taste test, chose Pepsi over rival Coca-Cola.

   a. 28-hour day
   b. 1990 Clean Air Act
   c. 33 Strategies of War
   d. Comparative advertising

2. A chief executive officer (_____) or chief executive is one of the highest-ranking corporate officer (executive) or administrator in charge of total management. An individual selected as President and _____ of a corporation, company, organization, or agency, reports to the board of directors. In internal communication and press releases, many companies capitalize the term and those of other high positions, even when they are not proper nouns.
   a. CEO
   b. Portfolio manager
   c. Chief executive officer
   d. Director of communications

3. A _____ is an entity formed between two or more parties to undertake economic activity together. The parties agree to create a new entity by both contributing equity, and they then share in the revenues, expenses, and control of the enterprise. The venture can be for one specific project only, or a continuing business relationship such as the Fuji Xerox _____.
   a. Civil Rights Act of 1991
   b. Meritor Savings Bank v. Vinson
   c. Patent
   d. Joint venture

4. _____ is the state or fact of exclusive rights and control over property, which may be an object, land/real estate or intellectual property. An _____ right is also referred to as title. The concept of _____ has existed for thousands of years and in all cultures.
   a. A4e
   b. A Stake in the Outcome
   c. Emanation of the state
   d. Ownership

5. An _____ is a person who has possession of an enterprise and assumes significant accountability for the inherent risks and the outcome. It is an ambitious leader who combines land, labor, and capital to create and market new goods or services. The term is a loanword from French and was first defined by the Irish economist Richard Cantillon.
   a. A4e
   b. AAAI
   c. A Stake in the Outcome
   d. Entrepreneur

6. _____ generally refers to a list of all planned expenses and revenues. It is a plan for saving and spending. A _____ is an important concept in microeconomics, which uses a _____ line to illustrate the trade-offs between two or more goods.
   a. 1990 Clean Air Act
   b. 33 Strategies of War
   c. 28-hour day
   d. Budget

Chapter 14. Ambulatory Care

7. In game theory, an _____ is a set of moves or strategies taken by the players, or their payoffs resulting from the actions or strategies taken by all players. The two are complementary in that given knowledge of the set of strategies of all players, the final state of the game is known, as are any relevant payoffs. In a game where chance or a random event is involved, the _____ is not known from only the set of strategies, but is only realized when the random event(s) are realized.
   a. A Stake in the Outcome
   b. A4e
   c. AAAI
   d. Outcome

8. In statistics, an _____ is an observation that is numerically distant from the rest of the data.

They can occur by chance in any distribution, but they are often indicative either of measurement error or that the population has a heavy-tailed distribution. In the former case one wishes to discard them or use statistics that are robust to _____s, while in the latter case they indicate that the distribution has high kurtosis and that one should be very cautious in using tool or intuitions that assume a normal distribution.

   a. A4e
   b. AAAI
   c. A Stake in the Outcome
   d. Outlier

9. In queueing theory, _____ is the proportion of the system's resources which is used by the traffic which arrives at it. It should be strictly less than one for the system to function well. It is usually represented by the symbol ρ.
   a. AAAI
   b. A Stake in the Outcome
   c. A4e
   d. Utilization

10. _____ is a business management strategy aimed at embedding awareness of quality in all organizational processes. _____ has been widely used in manufacturing, education, hospitals, call centers, government, and service industries, as well as NASA space and science programs.

As defined by the International Organization for Standardization (ISO):

> '_____ is a management approach for an organization, centered on quality, based on the participation of all its members and aiming at long-term success through customer satisfaction, and benefits to all members of the organization and to society.' ISO 8402:1994

One major aim is to reduce variation from every process so that greater consistency of effort is obtained. (Royse, D., Thyer, B., Padgett D., ' Logan T., 2006)

   a. Quality management
   b. 1990 Clean Air Act
   c. 28-hour day
   d. Total quality management

11. _____ can be considered to have three main components: quality control, quality assurance and quality improvement. _____ is focused not only on product quality, but also the means to achieve it. _____ therefore uses quality assurance and control of processes as well as products to achieve more consistent quality.
   a. 1990 Clean Air Act
   b. Total quality management
   c. Quality management
   d. 28-hour day

Chapter 15. Managed Health Care

1. _____ is an advertisement in which a particular product specifically mentions a competitor by name for the express purpose of showing why the competitor is inferior to the product naming it.

This should not be confused with parody advertisements, where a fictional product is being advertised for the purpose of poking fun at the particular advertisement, nor should it be confused with the use of a coined brand name for the purpose of comparing the product without actually naming an actual competitor. ('Wikipedia tastes better and is less filling than the Encyclopedia Galactica.')

In the 1980s, during what has been referred to as the cola wars, soft-drink manufacturer Pepsi ran a series of advertisements where people, caught on hidden camera, in a blind taste test, chose Pepsi over rival Coca-Cola.

   a. 1990 Clean Air Act
   b. Comparative advertising
   c. 33 Strategies of War
   d. 28-hour day

2. In economics, business, retail, and accounting, a _____ is the value of money that has been used up to produce something, and hence is not available for use anymore. In economics, a _____ is an alternative that is given up as a result of a decision. In business, the _____ may be one of acquisition, in which case the amount of money expended to acquire it is counted as _____.
   a. Fixed costs
   b. Cost overrun
   c. Cost
   d. Cost allocation

3. In decision theory and estimation theory, the _____ of an estimator, $\hat{\theta}$, of an unknown parameter of the distribution, θ, is the expected value of the loss function

$$R(\theta, \hat{\theta}) = \mathbb{E}_\theta L(\theta, \hat{\theta}) = \int L(\theta, \hat{\theta})\, dP_\theta.$$

where dP_θ is a probability measure parametrized by θ.

- For a scalar parameter θ and a quadratic loss function,

$$L(\theta, \hat{\theta}) = (\theta - \hat{\theta})^2$$

the _____ function becomes the mean squared error of the estimate,

$$R(\theta, \hat{\theta}) = E_\theta (\theta - \hat{\theta})^2$$

- In density estimation, the unknown parameter is probability density itself. The loss function is typically chosen to be a norm in an appropriate function space. For example, for L^2 norm,

$$L(f, \hat{f}) = \|f - \hat{f}\|_2^2$$

the _____ function becomes the mean integrated squared error

$$R(f, \hat{f}) = E\|f - \hat{f}\|^2$$

    a. Linear model   b. Financial modeling
    c. Risk aversion   d. Risk

4. The _____ (Pub.L. 93-406, 88 Stat. 829, enacted September 2, 1974) is an American federal statute that establishes minimum standards for pension plans in private industry and provides for extensive rules on the federal income tax effects of transactions associated with employee benefit plans.
    a. A Stake in the Outcome   b. A4e
    c. AAAI   d. Employee Retirement Income Security Act of 1974

5. _____ is the point where a person stops employment completely. A person may also semi-retire and keep some sort of _____ job, out of choice rather than necessity. This usually happens upon reaching a determined age, when physical conditions don't allow the person to work any more (by illness or accident), or even for personal choice (usually in the presence of an adequate pension or personal savings.)
    a. Termination of employment   b. Severance package
    c. Retirement   d. Wrongful dismissal

6. A _____ is defined as someone who controls access to something. It also refers to individuals who decide whether a given message will be distributed by a mass medium.

_____s serve several different purposes such as academic admissions, financial advising, and news editing.

a. 33 Strategies of War
b. 28-hour day
c. 1990 Clean Air Act
d. Gatekeeper

7. _____ of the learning curve effect and the closely related experience curve effect express the relationship between equations for experience and efficiency or between efficiency gains and investment in the effort. The experience of 'learning curves' was first observed by the 19th Century German psychologist Hermann Ebbinghaus according to the difficulty of memorizing varying numbers of verbal stimuli, and subsequent learning about the complex processes of learning are discussed in the

.

The rule used for representing the learning curve effect states that the more times a task has been performed, the less time will be required on each subsequent iteration.

a. Models
b. Point biserial correlation coefficient
c. Distribution
d. Spatial Decision Support Systems

8. An _____ is a sum paid by A to B by way of compensation for a particular loss suffered by B. The indemnifying party (A) may or may not be responsible for the loss suffered by the indemnified party (B.) Forms of _____ include cash payments, repairs, replacement, and reinstatement.

In common parlance, _____ is often used as a synonym for compensation or reparation.

a. AAAI
b. A4e
c. A Stake in the Outcome
d. Indemnity

9. _____ generally refers to a list of all planned expenses and revenues. It is a plan for saving and spending. A _____ is an important concept in microeconomics, which uses a _____ line to illustrate the trade-offs between two or more goods.

a. 33 Strategies of War
b. Budget
c. 1990 Clean Air Act
d. 28-hour day

10. A _____ is a form of periodic payment from an employer to an employee, which may be specified in an employment contract. It is contrasted with piece wages, where each job, hour or other unit is paid separately, rather than on a periodic basis.

From the point of a view of running a business, _____ can also be viewed as the cost of acquiring human resources for running operations, and is then termed personnel expense or _____ expense.

a. Human resource management
b. Human resources
c. Training and development
d. Salary

11. _____ is Latin for 'per day' or 'for each day'. It usually refers to the daily rate of any kind of payment. It may also refer to a specific amount of money that an organization allows an individual to spend per day, to cover living and traveling expenses in connection with work.

Chapter 15. Managed Health Care

a. Job security
c. Saint Monday
b. Per diem
d. Permatemp

12. _____ is one of the four Ps of the marketing mix. The other three aspects are product, promotion, and place. It is also a key variable in microeconomic price allocation theory.
   a. Price floor
   c. Transfer pricing
   b. Pricing
   d. Penetration pricing

13. _____ can be considered to have three main components: quality control, quality assurance and quality improvement. _____ is focused not only on product quality, but also the means to achieve it. _____ therefore uses quality assurance and control of processes as well as products to achieve more consistent quality.
   a. Quality management
   c. 28-hour day
   b. Total quality management
   d. 1990 Clean Air Act

14. In queueing theory, _____ is the proportion of the system's resources which is used by the traffic which arrives at it. It should be strictly less than one for the system to function well. It is usually represented by the symbol ρ.
   a. AAAI
   c. A Stake in the Outcome
   b. A4e
   d. Utilization

15. In economics, _____ is the desire to own something and the ability to pay for it. The term _____ signifies the ability or the willingness to buy a particular commodity at a given point of time.
   a. 33 Strategies of War
   c. 1990 Clean Air Act
   b. 28-hour day
   d. Demand

16. In economics, _____' is the art or science of controlling economic demand to avoid a recession. In natural resources management and environmental policy more generally, it refers to policies to control consumer demand for environmentally sensitive or harmful goods such as water and energy. Within manufacturing firms the term is used to describe the activities of demand forecasting, planning and order fulfillment.
   a. 28-hour day
   c. 33 Strategies of War
   b. Demand management
   d. 1990 Clean Air Act

17. _____ is a sub-topic of machine learning. It is 'the act of taking in raw data and taking an action based on the category of the data'. Most research in _____ is about methods for supervised learning and unsupervised learning.
   a. 33 Strategies of War
   c. 1990 Clean Air Act
   b. Pattern recognition
   d. 28-hour day

18. _____ is a broad label that refers to any individuals or households that use goods and services generated within the economy. The concept of a _____ is used in different contexts, so that the usage and significance of the term may vary.

Typically when business people and economists talk of _____s they are talking about person as _____, an aggregated commodity item with little individuality other than that expressed in the buy/not-buy decision.

Chapter 15. Managed Health Care

a. 1990 Clean Air Act
b. 28-hour day
c. Consumer
d. 33 Strategies of War

19. A _____ is typically described as a deliberate plan of action to guide decisions and achieve rational outcome(s.) However, the term may also be used to denote what is actually done, even though it is unplanned.

The term may apply to government, private sector organizations and groups, and individuals.

a. 1990 Clean Air Act
b. 33 Strategies of War
c. 28-hour day
d. Policy

20. _____ is a civil designation for persons who are incorporated in a fixed or permanent way to a society or group: regular member of the working staff, permanent staff distinguished from a supernumerary.

The term '_____' and its counterpart, 'supernumerary,' originated in Spanish and Latin American academy and government; it is now also used in countries all over the world, such as France, the U.S., England, Italy, etc.

There are _____ members of surgical organizations, of universities, of gastronomical associations, etc.

a. Abraham Harold Maslow
b. Adam Smith
c. Affiliation
d. Numerary

Chapter 16. Ethical Considerations in the Provision of Healthcare Services

1. _____ consists of the mental process of thinking involved with the process of judging the merits of multiple options and selecting one of them for action. Some simple examples include deciding whether to get up in the morning or go back to sleep, or selecting a given route for a journey. More complex examples (often decisions that affect what a person thinks or their core beliefs) include choosing a lifestyle, religious affiliation, or political position.

   a. Championship mobilization
   b. Trade study
   c. Choice
   d. Groups decision making

2. A _____ occurs when an individual or organization (such as a policeman, lawyer, insurance adjuster, politician, engineer, executive, director of a corporation, medical research scientist, physician, writer, editor, or any other entrusted individual or organization) has an interest that might compromise their actions. The presence of a _____ is independent from the execution of impropriety.

   In the legal profession, the duty of loyalty owed to a client prohibits an attorney (or a law firm) from representing any other party with interests adverse to those of a current client.

   a. 1990 Clean Air Act
   b. 28-hour day
   c. Global Corruption Report
   d. Conflict of interest

3. The _____ is an agency of the United States Department of Health and Human Services and is responsible for regulating and supervising the safety of foods, dietary supplements, drugs, vaccines, biological medical products, blood products, medical devices, radiation-emitting devices, veterinary products, and cosmetics. The FDA also enforces section 361 of the Public Health Service Act and the associated regulations, including sanitation requirements on interstate travel as well as specific rules for control of disease on products ranging from pet turtles to semen donations for assisted reproductive medicine techniques.

   The FDA is an agency within the United States Department of Health and Human Services responsible for protecting and promoting the nation's public health.

   a. Food and Drug Administration
   b. 1990 Clean Air Act
   c. 33 Strategies of War
   d. 28-hour day

4. _____ is an advertisement in which a particular product specifically mentions a competitor by name for the express purpose of showing why the competitor is inferior to the product naming it.

   This should not be confused with parody advertisements, where a fictional product is being advertised for the purpose of poking fun at the particular advertisement, nor should it be confused with the use of a coined brand name for the purpose of comparing the product without actually naming an actual competitor. ('Wikipedia tastes better and is less filling than the Encyclopedia Galactica.')

   In the 1980s, during what has been referred to as the cola wars, soft-drink manufacturer Pepsi ran a series of advertisements where people, caught on hidden camera, in a blind taste test, chose Pepsi over rival Coca-Cola.

   a. 1990 Clean Air Act
   b. 28-hour day
   c. 33 Strategies of War
   d. Comparative advertising

Chapter 16. Ethical Considerations in the Provision of Healthcare Services

5. In decision theory and estimation theory, the _____ of an estimator, $\hat{\theta}$, of an unknown parameter of the distribution, θ, is the expected value of the loss function

$$R(\theta, \hat{\theta}) = \mathbb{E}_\theta L(\theta, \hat{\theta}) = \int L(\theta, \hat{\theta}) \, dP_\theta.$$

where dP_θ is a probability measure parametrized by θ.

- For a scalar parameter θ and a quadratic loss function,

$$L(\theta, \hat{\theta}) = (\theta - \hat{\theta})^2$$

the _____ function becomes the mean squared error of the estimate,

$$R(\theta, \hat{\theta}) = E_\theta (\theta - \hat{\theta})^2$$

- In density estimation, the unknown parameter is probability density itself. The loss function is typically chosen to be a norm in an appropriate function space. For example, for L^2 norm,

$$L(f, \hat{f}) = \|f - \hat{f}\|_2^2$$

the _____ function becomes the mean integrated squared error

$$R(f, \hat{f}) = E\|f - \hat{f}\|^2$$

a. Risk
c. Financial modeling
b. Risk aversion
d. Linear model

6. The _____ is an American federal law which allows people who are not affiliated with the government to file actions against federal contractors claiming fraud against the government. The act of filing such actions is informally called 'whistleblowing.' Persons filing under the Act stand to receive a portion (usually about 15-25 percent) of any recovered damages.

a. Bennett Amendment
c. False Claims Act
b. Chrapliwy v. Uniroyal
d. Personal Responsibility and Work Opportunity Reconciliation Act

Chapter 17. Bioterrorism Preparedness

1. _____ is an advertisement in which a particular product specifically mentions a competitor by name for the express purpose of showing why the competitor is inferior to the product naming it.

This should not be confused with parody advertisements, where a fictional product is being advertised for the purpose of poking fun at the particular advertisement, nor should it be confused with the use of a coined brand name for the purpose of comparing the product without actually naming an actual competitor. ('Wikipedia tastes better and is less filling than the Encyclopedia Galactica.')

In the 1980s, during what has been referred to as the cola wars, soft-drink manufacturer Pepsi ran a series of advertisements where people, caught on hidden camera, in a blind taste test, chose Pepsi over rival Coca-Cola.

- a. 28-hour day
- b. 33 Strategies of War
- c. 1990 Clean Air Act
- d. Comparative advertising

2. _____ is one of the managerial functions like planning, organizing, staffing and directing. It is an important function because it helps to check the errors and to take the corrective action so that deviation from standards are minimized and stated goals of the organization are achieved in desired manner. According to modern concepts, _____ is a foreseeing action whereas earlier concept of _____ was used only when errors were detected. _____ in management means setting standards, measuring actual performance and taking corrective action.

- a. Turnover
- b. Schedule of reinforcement
- c. Decision tree pruning
- d. Control

Chapter 18. The History of Hospitals

1. A chief executive officer (_____) or chief executive is one of the highest-ranking corporate officer (executive) or administrator in charge of total management. An individual selected as President and _____ of a corporation, company, organization, or agency, reports to the board of directors. In internal communication and press releases, many companies capitalize the term and those of other high positions, even when they are not proper nouns.
   a. Director of communications
   b. Portfolio manager
   c. Chief executive officer
   d. CEO

2. _____ is an advertisement in which a particular product specifically mentions a competitor by name for the express purpose of showing why the competitor is inferior to the product naming it.

This should not be confused with parody advertisements, where a fictional product is being advertised for the purpose of poking fun at the particular advertisement, nor should it be confused with the use of a coined brand name for the purpose of comparing the product without actually naming an actual competitor. ('Wikipedia tastes better and is less filling than the Encyclopedia Galactica.')

In the 1980s, during what has been referred to as the cola wars, soft-drink manufacturer Pepsi ran a series of advertisements where people, caught on hidden camera, in a blind taste test, chose Pepsi over rival Coca-Cola.

   a. 33 Strategies of War
   b. 28-hour day
   c. 1990 Clean Air Act
   d. Comparative advertising

3. The _____ was a period in the late 18th and early 19th centuries when major changes in agriculture, manufacturing, mining, and transportation had a profound effect on the socioeconomic and cultural conditions in Britain. The changes subsequently spread throughout Europe, North America, and eventually the world. The onset of the _____ marked a major turning point in human society; almost every aspect of daily life was eventually influenced in some way.
   a. Abraham Harold Maslow
   b. Affiliation
   c. Adam Smith
   d. Industrial Revolution

4. _____ is the state or fact of exclusive rights and control over property, which may be an object, land/real estate or intellectual property. An _____ right is also referred to as title. The concept of _____ has existed for thousands of years and in all cultures.
   a. A4e
   b. Ownership
   c. A Stake in the Outcome
   d. Emanation of the state

5. _____ refers to the movement of cash into or out of a business or financial product. It is usually measured during a specified, finite period of time. Measurement of _____ can be used

   - to determine a project's rate of return or value. The time of _____s into and out of projects are used as inputs in financial models such as internal rate of return, and net present value.
   - to determine problems with a business's liquidity. Being profitable does not necessarily mean being liquid. A company can fail because of a shortage of cash, even while profitable.
   - as an alternate measure of a business's profits when it is believed that accrual accounting concepts do not represent economic realities. For example, a company may be notionally profitable but generating little operational cash (as may be the case for a company that barters its products rather than selling for cash.) In such a case, the company may be deriving additional operating cash by issuing shares evaluating default risk, re-investment requirements, etc.

_____ is a generic term used differently depending on the context. It may be defined by users for their own purposes.

a. Gross profit
c. Sweat equity

b. Gross profit margin
d. Cash flow

6. In microeconomics and management, the term _____ describes a style of management control. Vertically integrated companies are united through a hierarchy with a common owner. Usually each member of the hierarchy produces a different product or (market-specific) service, and the products combine to satisfy a common need.

a. 33 Strategies of War
c. 1990 Clean Air Act

b. 28-hour day
d. Vertical integration

Chapter 19. Hospital Organization and Management

1. _____ is an advertisement in which a particular product specifically mentions a competitor by name for the express purpose of showing why the competitor is inferior to the product naming it.

This should not be confused with parody advertisements, where a fictional product is being advertised for the purpose of poking fun at the particular advertisement, nor should it be confused with the use of a coined brand name for the purpose of comparing the product without actually naming an actual competitor. ('Wikipedia tastes better and is less filling than the Encyclopedia Galactica.')

In the 1980s, during what has been referred to as the cola wars, soft-drink manufacturer Pepsi ran a series of advertisements where people, caught on hidden camera, in a blind taste test, chose Pepsi over rival Coca-Cola.

a. 33 Strategies of War
b. Comparative advertising
c. 1990 Clean Air Act
d. 28-hour day

2. _____ is a term originating in military organization theory, but now used more commonly in business management, particularly human resource management. _____ refers to the number of subordinates a supervisor has.

In the hierarchical business organization of the past it was not uncommon to see average spans of 1 to 10 or even less. That is, one manager supervised ten employees on average.

a. Mentoring
b. Span of control
c. Senior management
d. CIFMS

3. _____ is one of the managerial functions like planning, organizing, staffing and directing. It is an important function because it helps to check the errors and to take the corrective action so that deviation from standards are minimized and stated goals of the organization are achieved in desired manner. According to modern concepts, _____ is a foreseeing action whereas earlier concept of _____ was used only when errors were detected. _____ in management means setting standards, measuring actual performance and taking corrective action.

a. Control
b. Decision tree pruning
c. Schedule of reinforcement
d. Turnover

4. In a military context, the _____ is the line of authority and responsibility along which orders are passed within a military unit and between different units. The term is also used in a civilian management context describing comparable hierarchical structures of authority.

a. 1990 Clean Air Act
b. Chain of command
c. French leave
d. 28-hour day

5. A _____ is a body of elected or appointed members who jointly oversee the activities of a company or organization. The body sometimes has a different name, such as board of trustees, board of governors, board of managers, or executive board. It is often simply referred to as 'the board.'

A board's activities are determined by the powers, duties, and responsibilities delegated to it or conferred on it by an authority outside itself.

a. Clean Water Act
b. Foreign Corrupt Practices Act
c. Competition law
d. Board of directors

Chapter 19. Hospital Organization and Management

6. _____ is a legal term that refers to a holder of property on behalf of a beneficiary. A trust can be set up either to benefit particular persons, or for any charitable purposes (but not generally for non-charitable purposes): typical examples are a will trust for the testator's children and family, a pension trust (to confer benefits on employees and their families), and a charitable trust. In all cases, the _____ may be a person or company, whether or not they are a prospective beneficiary.
   a. Trustee
   b. Design management
   c. Hierarchical organization
   d. Commercial management

7. A chief executive officer (_____) or chief executive is one of the highest-ranking corporate officer (executive) or administrator in charge of total management. An individual selected as President and _____ of a corporation, company, organization, or agency, reports to the board of directors. In internal communication and press releases, many companies capitalize the term and those of other high positions, even when they are not proper nouns.
   a. Director of communications
   b. Portfolio manager
   c. Chief executive officer
   d. CEO

8. A _____ or chief executive is one of the highest-ranking corporate officer (executive) or administrator in charge of total management. An individual selected as President and _____ of a corporation, company, organization, or agency, reports to the board of directors. In internal communication and press releases, many companies capitalize the term and those of other high positions, even when they are not proper nouns.
   a. Chief brand officer
   b. Purchasing manager
   c. Chief executive officer
   d. Financial analyst

9. While _____ literally refers to a person responsible for the performance of duties involved in running an organization, the exact meaning of the role is variable, depending on the organization.

While there is no clear line between executive or principal and inferior officers, principal officers are high-level officials in the executive branch of U.S. government such as department heads of independent agencies. In Humphrey's Executor v. United States, 295 U.S. 602 (1935), the Court distinguished between _____s and quasi-legislative or quasi-judicial officers by stating that the former serve at the pleasure of the President and may be removed at his discretion.

   a. Unreported employment
   b. Australian Fair Pay and Conditions Standard
   c. Easement
   d. Executive officer

10. _____ can refer to a law of local or limited application, passed under the authority of a higher law specifying what things may be regulated by the _____, or it can refer to the internal rules of a company or organisation.

Corporate and organizational _____s regulate only the organisation to which they apply and are generally concerned with the operation of the organisation, setting out the form, manner or procedure in which a company or organisation should be run. Corporate _____s are drafted by a corporation's founders or directors under the authority of its Charter or Articles of Incorporation.

   a. Fiduciary
   b. Bylaw
   c. Racketeer Influenced and Corrupt Organizations Act
   d. Genuine Occupational Qualification

11. A _____ is a list of the general tasks and responsibilities of a position. Typically, it also includes to whom the position reports, specifications such as the qualifications needed by the person in the job, salary range for the position, etc. A _____ is usually developed by conducting a job analysis, which includes examining the tasks and sequences of tasks necessary to perform the job.

   a. Recruitment

   b. Recruitment advertising

   c. Recruitment Process Insourcing

   d. Job description

Chapter 20. Patient Access Services: Into, Through, and Out of the Healthcare Process 89

1. _____ is an advertisement in which a particular product specifically mentions a competitor by name for the express purpose of showing why the competitor is inferior to the product naming it.

This should not be confused with parody advertisements, where a fictional product is being advertised for the purpose of poking fun at the particular advertisement, nor should it be confused with the use of a coined brand name for the purpose of comparing the product without actually naming an actual competitor. ('Wikipedia tastes better and is less filling than the Encyclopedia Galactica.')

In the 1980s, during what has been referred to as the cola wars, soft-drink manufacturer Pepsi ran a series of advertisements where people, caught on hidden camera, in a blind taste test, chose Pepsi over rival Coca-Cola.

   a. Comparative advertising
   b. 33 Strategies of War
   c. 1990 Clean Air Act
   d. 28-hour day

2. A _____ is a list of the general tasks and responsibilities of a position. Typically, it also includes to whom the position reports, specifications such as the qualifications needed by the person in the job, salary range for the position, etc. A _____ is usually developed by conducting a job analysis, which includes examining the tasks and sequences of tasks necessary to perform the job.
   a. Recruitment Process Insourcing
   b. Recruitment
   c. Job description
   d. Recruitment advertising

3. Advance health care directives are instructions given by individuals specifying what actions should be taken for their health in the event that they are no longer able to make decisions due to illness or incapacity. A _____ is one form of advance directive, leaving instructions for treatment. Another form authorises a specific type of power of attorney or health care proxy, where someone is appointed by the individual to make decisions on their behalf when they are incapacitated.
   a. 28-hour day
   b. 33 Strategies of War
   c. 1990 Clean Air Act
   d. Living will

4. The _____ resulted in the passing of two bills: Medicare and Medicaid. The act provided federal health insurance for the elderly (over 65) and for poor families. While Lyndon B. Johnson (LBJ) was responsible for signing the bill, there were many others involved in drafting the final bill that was introduced to the United States Congress in March 1965.
   a. Guarantee
   b. Social Security Act of 1965
   c. Civil Rights Act of 1964
   d. Bylaw

5. _____ is defined as free choice of one's own acts without external compulsion; and especially as the freedom of the people of a given territory to determine their own political status or independence from their current state. In other words, it is the right of the people of a certain nation to decide how they want to be governed without the influence of any other country. The latter is a complex concept with conflicting definitions and legal criteria for determining which groups may legitimately claim the right to _____..
   a. Populism
   b. 1990 Clean Air Act
   c. Self-Determination
   d. 28-hour day

6. In queueing theory, _____ is the proportion of the system's resources which is used by the traffic which arrives at it. It should be strictly less than one for the system to function well. It is usually represented by the symbol ρ.
   a. A4e
   b. Utilization
   c. A Stake in the Outcome
   d. AAAI

Chapter 20. Patient Access Services: Into, Through, and Out of the Healthcare Process

7. A _____ is typically described as a deliberate plan of action to guide decisions and achieve rational outcome(s.) However, the term may also be used to denote what is actually done, even though it is unplanned.

The term may apply to government, private sector organizations and groups, and individuals.

a. 28-hour day
b. 1990 Clean Air Act
c. Policy
d. 33 Strategies of War

8. _____ refers to planned and systematic production processes that provide confidence in a product's suitability for its intended purpose. Refer to the definition by Merriam-Webster for further information. It is a set of activities intended to ensure that products (goods and/or services) satisfy customer requirements in a systematic, reliable fashion.

a. 28-hour day
b. Risk assessment
c. Quality Assurance
d. 1990 Clean Air Act

9. _____ is a business management strategy aimed at embedding awareness of quality in all organizational processes. _____ has been widely used in manufacturing, education, hospitals, call centers, government, and service industries, as well as NASA space and science programs.

As defined by the International Organization for Standardization (ISO):

'_____ is a management approach for an organization, centered on quality, based on the participation of all its members and aiming at long-term success through customer satisfaction, and benefits to all members of the organization and to society.' ISO 8402:1994

One major aim is to reduce variation from every process so that greater consistency of effort is obtained. (Royse, D., Thyer, B., Padgett D., ' Logan T., 2006)

a. Quality management
b. 1990 Clean Air Act
c. 28-hour day
d. Total quality management

10. _____ can be considered to have three main components: quality control, quality assurance and quality improvement. _____ is focused not only on product quality, but also the means to achieve it. _____ therefore uses quality assurance and control of processes as well as products to achieve more consistent quality.

a. 28-hour day
b. 1990 Clean Air Act
c. Total quality management
d. Quality management

Chapter 21. Laboratories

1. In economics, business, retail, and accounting, a _____ is the value of money that has been used up to produce something, and hence is not available for use anymore. In economics, a _____ is an alternative that is given up as a result of a decision. In business, the _____ may be one of acquisition, in which case the amount of money expended to acquire it is counted as _____.
   - a. Cost allocation
   - b. Fixed costs
   - c. Cost overrun
   - d. Cost

2. In management accounting, _____ establishes budget and actual cost of operations, processes, departments or product and the analysis of variances, profitability or social use of funds. Managers use _____ to support decision-making to cut a company's costs and improve profitability. As a form of management accounting, _____ need not follow standards such as GAAP, because its primary use is for internal managers, rather than outside users, and what to compute is instead decided pragmatically.
   - a. Marginal cost
   - b. Transaction cost
   - c. Quality costs
   - d. Cost accounting

3. In queueing theory, _____ is the proportion of the system's resources which is used by the traffic which arrives at it. It should be strictly less than one for the system to function well. It is usually represented by the symbol ρ.
   - a. Utilization
   - b. A Stake in the Outcome
   - c. A4e
   - d. AAAI

4. _____ refers to training in different ways to improve overall performance. It takes advantage of the particular effectiveness of each training method, while at the same time attempting to neglect the shortcomings of that method by combining it with other methods that address its weaknesses.

   Cross training is employee-employer field means, training employees to do one another's work.

   - a. Cross-training
   - b. 1990 Clean Air Act
   - c. 33 Strategies of War
   - d. 28-hour day

5. _____ is an advertisement in which a particular product specifically mentions a competitor by name for the express purpose of showing why the competitor is inferior to the product naming it.

   This should not be confused with parody advertisements, where a fictional product is being advertised for the purpose of poking fun at the particular advertisement, nor should it be confused with the use of a coined brand name for the purpose of comparing the product without actually naming an actual competitor. ('Wikipedia tastes better and is less filling than the Encyclopedia Galactica.')

   In the 1980s, during what has been referred to as the cola wars, soft-drink manufacturer Pepsi ran a series of advertisements where people, caught on hidden camera, in a blind taste test, chose Pepsi over rival Coca-Cola.

   - a. 33 Strategies of War
   - b. 1990 Clean Air Act
   - c. 28-hour day
   - d. Comparative advertising

6. Business _____ is the process a business uses to contain costs. It consists of integrating applications, cutting labor wherever possible, and using software applications throughout the organization.

   There are four main techniques for delivering automation of a process.

a. Sensitivity analysis
b. Process automation
c. Business process reengineering
d. Procurement

7. _____ is the use of control systems (such as numerical control, programmable logic control, and other industrial control systems), in concert with other applications of information technology (such as computer-aided technologies [CAD, CAM, CAx]), to control industrial machinery and processes, reducing the need for human intervention. In the scope of industrialization, _____ is a step beyond mechanization. Whereas mechanization provided human operators with machinery to assist them with the physical requirements of work, _____ greatly reduces the need for human sensory and mental requirements as well.
   a. AAAI
   b. Automation
   c. A Stake in the Outcome
   d. A4e

8. _____ is a cross-disciplinary area concerned with protecting the safety, health and welfare of people engaged in work or employment. The goal of all _____ programs is to foster a work free safe environment. As a secondary effect, it may also protect co-workers, family members, employers, customers, suppliers, nearby communities, and other members of the public who are impacted by the workplace environment.
   a. A4e
   b. Occupational Safety and Health
   c. AAAI
   d. A Stake in the Outcome

9. The United States _____ is an agency of the United States Department of Labor. It was created by Congress under the Occupational Safety and Health Act, signed by President Richard M. Nixon, on December 29, 1970. Its mission is to prevent work-related injuries, illnesses, and deaths by issuing and enforcing rules (called standards) for workplace safety and health.
   a. Operant conditioning
   b. Unemployment insurance
   c. Occupational Safety and Health Administration
   d. Opinion leadership

10. _____ is an organization's process of defining its strategy and making decisions on allocating its resources to pursue this strategy, including its capital and people. Various business analysis techniques can be used in _____, including SWOT analysis (Strengths, Weaknesses, Opportunities, and Threats) and PEST analysis (Political, Economic, Social, and Technological analysis) or STEER analysis involving Socio-cultural, Technological, Economic, Ecological, and Regulatory factors and EPISTEL (Environment, Political, Informatic, Social, Technological, Economic and Legal)

_____ is the formal consideration of an organization's future course. All _____ deals with at least one of three key questions:

1. 'What do we do?'
2. 'For whom do we do it?'
3. 'How do we excel?'

In business _____, the third question is better phrased 'How can we beat or avoid competition?'. (Bradford and Duncan, page 1.)

   a. 1990 Clean Air Act
   b. Strategic planning
   c. 33 Strategies of War
   d. 28-hour day

11. A _____ is an entity formed between two or more parties to undertake economic activity together. The parties agree to create a new entity by both contributing equity, and they then share in the revenues, expenses, and control of the enterprise. The venture can be for one specific project only, or a continuing business relationship such as the Fuji Xerox _____.
   a. Civil Rights Act of 1991
   b. Meritor Savings Bank v. Vinson
   c. Patent
   d. Joint venture

12. An _____ is a person who has possession of an enterprise and assumes significant accountability for the inherent risks and the outcome. It is an ambitious leader who combines land, labor, and capital to create and market new goods or services. The term is a loanword from French and was first defined by the Irish economist Richard Cantillon.
   a. A4e
   b. AAAI
   c. A Stake in the Outcome
   d. Entrepreneur

Chapter 22. Pharmacy

1. _____ is technology based on biology, especially when used in agriculture, food science, and medicine. United Nations Convention on Biological Diversity defines _____ as:

_____ is often used to refer to genetic engineering technology of the 21st century, however the term encompasses a wider range and history of procedures for modifying biological organisms according to the needs of humanity, going back to the initial modifications of native plants into improved food crops through artificial selection and hybridization. Bioengineering is the science upon which all biotechnological applications are based.

a. 28-hour day
c. 1990 Clean Air Act
b. 33 Strategies of War
d. Biotechnology

2. _____ is an advertisement in which a particular product specifically mentions a competitor by name for the express purpose of showing why the competitor is inferior to the product naming it.

This should not be confused with parody advertisements, where a fictional product is being advertised for the purpose of poking fun at the particular advertisement, nor should it be confused with the use of a coined brand name for the purpose of comparing the product without actually naming an actual competitor. ('Wikipedia tastes better and is less filling than the Encyclopedia Galactica.')

In the 1980s, during what has been referred to as the cola wars, soft-drink manufacturer Pepsi ran a series of advertisements where people, caught on hidden camera, in a blind taste test, chose Pepsi over rival Coca-Cola.

a. 1990 Clean Air Act
c. 28-hour day
b. 33 Strategies of War
d. Comparative advertising

3. In economics, business, retail, and accounting, a _____ is the value of money that has been used up to produce something, and hence is not available for use anymore. In economics, a _____ is an alternative that is given up as a result of a decision. In business, the _____ may be one of acquisition, in which case the amount of money expended to acquire it is counted as _____.

a. Fixed costs
c. Cost overrun
b. Cost allocation
d. Cost

4. A _____ is one scenario provided for evaluation by respondents in a Choice Experiment. Responses are collected and used to create a Choice Model. Respondents are usually provided with a series of differing _____s for evaluation.

a. Choice Set
c. Computerized classification test
b. Pairwise comparison
d. Thurstone scale

5. In game theory, an _____ is a set of moves or strategies taken by the players, or their payoffs resulting from the actions or strategies taken by all players. The two are complementary in that given knowledge of the set of strategies of all players, the final state of the game is known, as are any relevant payoffs. In a game where chance or a random event is involved, the _____ is not known from only the set of strategies, but is only realized when the random event(s) are realized.

a. AAAI
c. A4e
b. A Stake in the Outcome
d. Outcome

Chapter 22. Pharmacy

6. _____ has been described as the 'process of social influence in which one person can enlist the aid and support of others in the accomplishment of a common task' . A definition more inclusive of followers comes from Alan Keith of Genentech who said '_____ is ultimately about creating a way for people to contribute to making something extraordinary happen.'

_____ is one of the most salient aspects of the organizational context. However, defining _____ has been challenging.

   a. Leadership
   b. Situational leadership
   c. 1990 Clean Air Act
   d. 28-hour day

7. A _____ is a list of the general tasks and responsibilities of a position. Typically, it also includes to whom the position reports, specifications such as the qualifications needed by the person in the job, salary range for the position, etc. A _____ is usually developed by conducting a job analysis, which includes examining the tasks and sequences of tasks necessary to perform the job.
   a. Recruitment Process Insourcing
   b. Job description
   c. Recruitment advertising
   d. Recruitment

8. _____ is one of the four elements of marketing mix. An organization or set of organizations (go-betweens) involved in the process of making a product or service available for use or consumption by a consumer or business user.

The other three parts of the marketing mix are product, pricing, and promotion.

   a. Job creation programs
   b. Matching theory
   c. Missing completely at random
   d. Distribution

9. The _____ of a product is the cost per standard unit supplied, which may be a single sample or a container of a given number. When purchasing more than a single unit, the total cost will increase with the number of units, but it is common for the _____ to decrease as quantity is increased (bulk purchasing), as there are discounts etc. This reduction in long run _____s which arise from an increase in production/purchasing is due to the fixed costs being spread out over more products and is called economies of scale.
   a. Unit cost
   b. A Stake in the Outcome
   c. AAAI
   d. A4e

10. _____ refers to metrics and measures of output from production processes, per unit of input. Labor _____, for example, is typically measured as a ratio of output per labor-hour, an input. _____ may be conceived of as a metrics of the technical or engineering efficiency of production.
    a. Master production schedule
    b. Remanufacturing
    c. Productivity
    d. Value engineering

11. The maturity road mapping method (MRMM) is a general procedure to increase the speed and reduce the cost of achieving the maturity condition in a process, product or an organization and with similar approach like PDCA and we call it as _____.

This methodology was developed from 1985 and completed during more than two decades. The basic elements of this model are three as follows; 1- software 2- hardware 3- roadware

Book over of MRM Components of economic growth through productivity (Saari 2006)

The logical manner of this approach is like the periodic table of the chemical elements(by Dmitri Mendeleev) that with defining the trend of electron circulation around cell of the atom helps understanding and predicting unknown atoms.

    a. Perfect competition
    b. Deflation
    c. Gross domestic product
    d. Productivity management

12. _____ is the process of comparing the cost, cycle time, productivity, or quality of a specific process or method to another that is widely considered to be an industry standard or best practice. Essentially, _____ provides a snapshot of the performance of your business and helps you understand where you are in relation to a particular standard. The result is often a business case for making changes in order to make improvements.

    a. Cost leadership
    b. Complementors
    c. Benchmarking
    d. Competitive heterogeneity

13. A _____ is the belief that there is a technique, method, process, activity, incentive or reward that is more effective at delivering a particular outcome than any other technique, method, process, etc. The idea is that with proper processes, checks, and testing, a desired outcome can be delivered with fewer problems and unforeseen complications. _____s can also be defined as the most efficient (least amount of effort) and effective (best results) way of accomplishing a task, based on repeatable procedures that have proven themselves over time for large numbers of people.

    a. Hierarchical organization
    b. Fix it twice
    c. Best practice
    d. Design management

14. _____ is one of the managerial functions like planning, organizing, staffing and directing. It is an important function because it helps to check the errors and to take the corrective action so that deviation from standards are minimized and stated goals of the organization are achieved in desired manner.According to modern concepts, _____ is a foreseeing action whereas earlier concept of _____ was used only when errors were detected. _____ in management means setting standards, measuring actual performance and taking corrective action.

    a. Schedule of reinforcement
    b. Turnover
    c. Decision tree pruning
    d. Control

15. A _____ is a set of exclusive rights granted by a state to an inventor or his assignee for a limited period of time in exchange for a disclosure of an invention.

The procedure for granting _____s, the requirements placed on the _____ee and the extent of the exclusive rights vary widely between countries according to national laws and international agreements. Typically, however, a _____ application must include one or more claims defining the invention which must be new, inventive, and useful or industrially applicable.

a. Food, Drug, and Cosmetic Act
b. Labor Management Reporting and Disclosure Act
c. Federal Trade Commission Act
d. Patent

16. The _____ of 1936 (or Anti-Price Discrimination Act, 15 U.S.C. § 13) is a United States federal law that prohibits what were considered, at the time of passage, to be anticompetitive practices by producers, specifically price discrimination. It grew out of practices in which chain stores were allowed to purchase goods at lower prices than other retailers.

a. Privity
b. Robinson-Patman Act
c. Labor Management Reporting and Disclosure Act
d. Bona fide occupational qualification

Chapter 23. Material and Resource Management

1. In economics, business, retail, and accounting, a _____ is the value of money that has been used up to produce something, and hence is not available for use anymore. In economics, a _____ is an alternative that is given up as a result of a decision. In business, the _____ may be one of acquisition, in which case the amount of money expended to acquire it is counted as _____.

   a. Cost
   b. Cost overrun
   c. Cost allocation
   d. Fixed costs

2. _____ is the branch of logistics that deals with the tangible components of a supply chain. Specifically, this covers the acquisition of spare parts and replacements, quality control of purchasing and ordering such parts, and the standards involved in ordering, shipping, and warehousing the said parts.

   A large component of _____ is ensuring that parts and materials used in the supply chain meet minimum requirements by performing quality assurance (QA.)

   a. Vendor Managed Inventory
   b. Materials management
   c. Delayed differentiation
   d. Supply-Chain Operations Reference

3. A _____ is the system of organizations, people, technology, activities, information and resources involved in moving a product or service from supplier to customer. _____ activities transform natural resources, raw materials and components into a finished product that is delivered to the end customer. In sophisticated _____ systems, used products may re-enter the _____ at any point where residual value is recyclable.

   a. Wholesalers
   b. Packaging
   c. Drop shipping
   d. Supply chain

4. _____ is an advertisement in which a particular product specifically mentions a competitor by name for the express purpose of showing why the competitor is inferior to the product naming it.

   This should not be confused with parody advertisements, where a fictional product is being advertised for the purpose of poking fun at the particular advertisement, nor should it be confused with the use of a coined brand name for the purpose of comparing the product without actually naming an actual competitor. ('Wikipedia tastes better and is less filling than the Encyclopedia Galactica.')

   In the 1980s, during what has been referred to as the cola wars, soft-drink manufacturer Pepsi ran a series of advertisements where people, caught on hidden camera, in a blind taste test, chose Pepsi over rival Coca-Cola.

   a. 28-hour day
   b. 1990 Clean Air Act
   c. 33 Strategies of War
   d. Comparative advertising

5. _____ is one of the four elements of marketing mix. An organization or set of organizations (go-betweens) involved in the process of making a product or service available for use or consumption by a consumer or business user.

   The other three parts of the marketing mix are product, pricing, and promotion.

   a. Job creation programs
   b. Matching theory
   c. Missing completely at random
   d. Distribution

Chapter 23. Material and Resource Management

6. A _____ is an invitation for suppliers, often through a bidding process, to submit a proposal on a specific commodity or service. A bidding process is one of the best methods for leveraging a company's negotiating ability and purchasing power with suppliers. The _____ process brings structure to the procurement decision and allows the risks and benefits to be identified clearly upfront.
   - a. 1990 Clean Air Act
   - b. Request for proposal
   - c. Lead generation
   - d. Lead management

7. In a human resources context, _____ or labor _____ is the rate at which an employer gains and loses employees. Simple ways to describe it are 'how long employees tend to stay' or 'the rate of traffic through the revolving door.' _____ is measured for individual companies and for their industry as a whole. If an employer is said to have a high _____ relative to its competitors, it means that employees of that company have a shorter average tenure than those of other companies in the same industry.
   - a. Ten year occupational employment projection
   - b. Career portfolios
   - c. Continuous
   - d. Turnover

8. _____ is one of the managerial functions like planning, organizing, staffing and directing. It is an important function because it helps to check the errors and to take the corrective action so that deviation from standards are minimized and stated goals of the organization are achieved in desired manner. According to modern concepts, _____ is a foreseeing action whereas earlier concept of _____ was used only when errors were detected. _____ in management means setting standards, measuring actual performance and taking corrective action.
   - a. Control
   - b. Turnover
   - c. Schedule of reinforcement
   - d. Decision tree pruning

9. _____ is the level of inventory that minimizes the total inventory holding costs and ordering costs. The framework used to determine this order quantity is also known as Wilson _____ Model. The model was developed by F. W. Harris in 1913.
   - a. Economic order quantity
   - b. Effective executive
   - c. Event management
   - d. Anti-leadership

10. In business management, _____ is money spent to keep and maintain a stock of goods in storage.

   The most obvious _____s include rent for the required space; equipment, materials, and labor to operate the space; insurance; security; interest on money invested in the inventory and space, and other direct expenses. Some stored goods become obsolete before they are sold, reducing their contribution to revenue while having no effect on their _____.

   - a. Private placement
   - b. Choquet integral
   - c. Market niche
   - d. Holding cost

11. The _____ is the level of inventory when a fresh order should be made with suppliers to bring the inventory up by the Economic order quantity ('EOQ'.)

   The _____ for replenishment of stock occurs when the level of inventory drops down to zero. In view of instantaneous replenishment of stock the level of inventory jumps to the original level from zero level.

a. 1990 Clean Air Act
b. 28-hour day
c. Finished goods
d. Reorder point

12. The _____ of a product is the cost per standard unit supplied, which may be a single sample or a container of a given number. When purchasing more than a single unit, the total cost will increase with the number of units, but it is common for the _____ to decrease as quantity is increased (bulk purchasing), as there are discounts etc. This reduction in long run _____s which arise from an increase in production/purchasing is due to the fixed costs being spread out over more products and is called economies of scale.

a. Unit cost
b. A Stake in the Outcome
c. AAAI
d. A4e

13. The term '_____' refers to the concept of collecting information and attempting to spot a pattern in the information. In some fields of study, the term '_____' has more formally-defined meanings.

In project management _____ is a mathematical technique that uses historical results to predict future outcome.

a. Stepwise regression
b. Trend analysis
c. Least squares
d. Regression analysis

Chapter 24. Designing and Implementing a Hospital Compliance Program

1. _____ is an advertisement in which a particular product specifically mentions a competitor by name for the express purpose of showing why the competitor is inferior to the product naming it.

This should not be confused with parody advertisements, where a fictional product is being advertised for the purpose of poking fun at the particular advertisement, nor should it be confused with the use of a coined brand name for the purpose of comparing the product without actually naming an actual competitor. ('Wikipedia tastes better and is less filling than the Encyclopedia Galactica.')

In the 1980s, during what has been referred to as the cola wars, soft-drink manufacturer Pepsi ran a series of advertisements where people, caught on hidden camera, in a blind taste test, chose Pepsi over rival Coca-Cola.

 a. Comparative advertising
 b. 1990 Clean Air Act
 c. 33 Strategies of War
 d. 28-hour day

2. The _____ is an American federal law which allows people who are not affiliated with the government to file actions against federal contractors claiming fraud against the government. The act of filing such actions is informally called 'whistleblowing.' Persons filing under the Act stand to receive a portion (usually about 15-25 percent) of any recovered damages.

 a. Bennett Amendment
 b. Personal Responsibility and Work Opportunity Reconciliation Act
 c. Chrapliwy v. Uniroyal
 d. False Claims Act

3. The _____ duty is a legal relationship of confidence or trust between two or more parties, most commonly a _____ or trustee and a principal or beneficiary. One party, for example a corporate trust company or the trust department of a bank, holds a _____ relation or acts in a _____ capacity to another, such as one whose funds are entrusted to it for investment. In a _____ relation one person justifiably reposes confidence, good faith, reliance and trust in another whose aid, advice or protection is sought in some matter.

 a. Copyright Act of 1976
 b. Corporate governance
 c. Fiduciary
 d. Last Injurious Exposure Rule

4. _____ is a process for determining and addressing needs, or gaps between current conditions and desired conditions organizations it is known as community needs analysis. It involves identifying material problems/deficits/weaknesses and advantages/opportunites/strengths, and evaluating possible solutions that take those qualities into consideration.

 a. Needs assessment
 b. 33 Strategies of War
 c. 1990 Clean Air Act
 d. 28-hour day

5. Quality management can be considered to have three main components: quality control, quality assurance and _____. Quality management is focused not only on product quality, but also the means to achieve it. Quality management therefore uses quality assurance and control of processes as well as products to achieve more consistent quality.

 a. 28-hour day
 b. Quality management
 c. 1990 Clean Air Act
 d. Quality improvement

Chapter 24. Designing and Implementing a Hospital Compliance Program

6. The general definition of an _____ is an evaluation of a person, organization, system, process, project or product. _____s are performed to ascertain the validity and reliability of information; also to provide an assessment of a system's internal control. The goal of an _____ is to express an opinion on the person / organization/system (etc) in question, under evaluation based on work done on a test basis.
   a. A Stake in the Outcome
   b. Audit committee
   c. Internal control
   d. Audit

7. In decision theory and estimation theory, the _____ of an estimator, $\hat{\theta}$, of an unknown parameter of the distribution, θ, is the expected value of the loss function

$$R(\theta, \hat{\theta}) = \mathbb{E}_\theta L(\theta, \hat{\theta}) = \int L(\theta, \hat{\theta})\, dP_\theta.$$

where dP_θ is a probability measure parametrized by θ.

- For a scalar parameter θ and a quadratic loss function,

$$L(\theta, \hat{\theta}) = (\theta - \hat{\theta})^2$$

the _____ function becomes the mean squared error of the estimate,

$$R(\theta, \hat{\theta}) = E_\theta (\theta - \hat{\theta})^2$$

- In density estimation, the unknown parameter is probability density itself. The loss function is typically chosen to be a norm in an appropriate function space. For example, for L^2 norm,

$$L(f, \hat{f}) = \|f - \hat{f}\|_2^2$$

the _____ function becomes the mean integrated squared error

$$R(f, \hat{f}) = E\|f - \hat{f}\|^2$$

   a. Linear model
   b. Risk aversion
   c. Financial modeling
   d. Risk

8. _____ is a step in a risk management process. _____ is the determination of quantitative or qualitative value of risk related to a concrete situation and a recognized threat (also called hazard.) Quantitative _____ requires calculations of two components of risk: R, the magnitude of the potential loss L, and the probability p, that the loss will occur.
   a. 28-hour day
   b. 1990 Clean Air Act
   c. Risk assessment
   d. Quality assurance

Chapter 24. Designing and Implementing a Hospital Compliance Program   103

9. A chief executive officer (_____) or chief executive is one of the highest-ranking corporate officer (executive) or administrator in charge of total management. An individual selected as President and _____ of a corporation, company, organization, or agency, reports to the board of directors. In internal communication and press releases, many companies capitalize the term and those of other high positions, even when they are not proper nouns.

   a. Chief executive officer
   b. CEO
   c. Portfolio manager
   d. Director of communications

10. A _____ is a change implemented to address a weakness identified in a management system. Normally _____s are implemented in response to a customer complaint, abnormal levels of internal nonconformity, nonconformities identified during an internal audit or adverse or unstable trends in product and process monitoring such as would be identified by SPC.

    The process of determining a _____ requires identification of actions that can be taken to prevent or mitigate the weakness.

   a. Corrective action
   b. 28-hour day
   c. 1990 Clean Air Act
   d. Zero defects

11. The _____ of 1990 (ADA) is the short title of United States (Pub.L. 101-336, 104 Stat. 327, enacted July 26, 1990), codified at 42 U.S.C. § 12101 et seq. It was signed into law on July 26, 1990, by President George H. W. Bush, and later amended with changes effective January 1, 2009. The ADA is a wide-ranging civil rights law that prohibits, under certain circumstances, discrimination based on disability. It affords similar protections against discrimination to Americans with disabilities as the Civil Rights Act of 1964,

   a. Equal Pay Act of 1963
   b. Australian labour law
   c. Employment discrimination
   d. Americans with Disabilities Act

12. The U.S. _____ of 1973 prohibits discrimination on the basis of disability in programs conducted by Federal agencies, in programs receiving Federal financial assistance, in Federal employment, and in the employment practices of Federal contractors. The standards for determining employment discrimination under the _____ are the same as those used in title I of the Americans with Disabilities Act.

    There are four key sections of the Act.

   a. 33 Strategies of War
   b. 1990 Clean Air Act
   c. 28-hour day
   d. Rehabilitation Act

Chapter 25. Quality Assurance and Improvement

1. _____ refers to planned and systematic production processes that provide confidence in a product's suitability for its intended purpose. Refer to the definition by Merriam-Webster for further information . It is a set of activities intended to ensure that products (goods and/or services) satisfy customer requirements in a systematic, reliable fashion.
   a. 1990 Clean Air Act
   b. Risk assessment
   c. 28-hour day
   d. Quality assurance

2. _____ is the process of subjecting an author's scholarly work, research, or ideas to the scrutiny of others who are experts in the same field. _____ requires a community of experts in a given field, who are qualified and able to perform impartial review. Impartial review, especially of work in less narrowly defined or inter-disciplinary fields, may be difficult to accomplish; and the significance of an idea may never be widely appreciated among its contemporaries.
   a. 33 Strategies of War
   b. 28-hour day
   c. Peer review
   d. 1990 Clean Air Act

3. _____ is an advertisement in which a particular product specifically mentions a competitor by name for the express purpose of showing why the competitor is inferior to the product naming it.

   This should not be confused with parody advertisements, where a fictional product is being advertised for the purpose of poking fun at the particular advertisement, nor should it be confused with the use of a coined brand name for the purpose of comparing the product without actually naming an actual competitor. ('Wikipedia tastes better and is less filling than the Encyclopedia Galactica.')

   In the 1980s, during what has been referred to as the cola wars, soft-drink manufacturer Pepsi ran a series of advertisements where people, caught on hidden camera, in a blind taste test, chose Pepsi over rival Coca-Cola.

   a. 1990 Clean Air Act
   b. 33 Strategies of War
   c. Comparative advertising
   d. 28-hour day

4. A _____ is one scenario provided for evaluation by respondents in a Choice Experiment. Responses are collected and used to create a Choice Model. Respondents are usually provided with a series of differing _____s for evaluation.
   a. Computerized classification test
   b. Thurstone scale
   c. Pairwise comparison
   d. Choice Set

5. _____ is the principle that the government must respect all of the legal rights that are owed to a person according to the law of the land. As developed through a large body of case law in the United States, this principle gives individuals a varying ability to enforce their rights against alleged violations by governments and their agents (that is, state actors), but normally not against other private citizens.

   _____ has also been frequently interpreted as placing limitations on laws and legal proceedings, in order for judges instead of legislators to define and guarantee fundamental fairness, justice, and liberty.

   a. Clayton Antitrust Act
   b. Sick leave
   c. Maximum medical improvement
   d. Due process

6. Quality management can be considered to have three main components: quality control, quality assurance and _____. Quality management is focused not only on product quality, but also the means to achieve it. Quality management therefore uses quality assurance and control of processes as well as products to achieve more consistent quality.

Chapter 25. Quality Assurance and Improvement

a. Quality Improvement
b. Quality management
c. 28-hour day
d. 1990 Clean Air Act

7. _____ is a cross-disciplinary area concerned with protecting the safety, health and welfare of people engaged in work or employment. The goal of all _____ programs is to foster a work free safe environment. As a secondary effect, it may also protect co-workers, family members, employers, customers, suppliers, nearby communities, and other members of the public who are impacted by the workplace environment.
   a. AAAI
   b. Occupational Safety and Health
   c. A Stake in the Outcome
   d. A4e

8. The United States _____ is an agency of the United States Department of Labor. It was created by Congress under the Occupational Safety and Health Act, signed by President Richard M. Nixon, on December 29, 1970. Its mission is to prevent work-related injuries, illnesses, and deaths by issuing and enforcing rules (called standards) for workplace safety and health.
   a. Unemployment insurance
   b. Operant conditioning
   c. Opinion leadership
   d. Occupational Safety and Health Administration

9. In engineering and manufacturing, _____ and quality engineering are used in developing systems to ensure products or services are designed and produced to meet or exceed customer requirements. Refer to the definition by Merriam-Webster for further information . These systems are often developed in conjunction with other business and engineering disciplines using a cross-functional approach.
   a. Single Minute Exchange of Die
   b. Process capability
   c. Statistical process control
   d. Quality control

10. _____ is one of the managerial functions like planning, organizing, staffing and directing. It is an important function because it helps to check the errors and to take the corrective action so that deviation from standards are minimized and stated goals of the organization are achieved in desired manner.According to modern concepts, _____ is a foreseeing action whereas earlier concept of _____ was used only when errors were detected. _____ in management means setting standards, measuring actual performance and taking corrective action.
    a. Control
    b. Turnover
    c. Schedule of reinforcement
    d. Decision tree pruning

11. _____ is the process of comparing the cost, cycle time, productivity, or quality of a specific process or method to another that is widely considered to be an industry standard or best practice. Essentially, _____ provides a snapshot of the performance of your business and helps you understand where you are in relation to a particular standard. The result is often a business case for making changes in order to make improvements.
    a. Cost leadership
    b. Complementors
    c. Competitive heterogeneity
    d. Benchmarking

12. A _____ is the belief that there is a technique, method, process, activity, incentive or reward that is more effective at delivering a particular outcome than any other technique, method, process, etc. The idea is that with proper processes, checks, and testing, a desired outcome can be delivered with fewer problems and unforeseen complications. _____s can also be defined as the most efficient (least amount of effort) and effective (best results) way of accomplishing a task, based on repeatable procedures that have proven themselves over time for large numbers of people.

a. Fix it twice
b. Best practice
c. Hierarchical organization
d. Design management

13. In probability theory, a probability distribution is called _____ if its cumulative distribution function is _____. This is equivalent to saying that for random variables X with the distribution in question, Pr[X = a] = 0 for all real numbers a, i.e.: the probability that X attains the value a is zero, for any number a. If the distribution of X is _____ then X is called a _____ random variable.

a. Decision tree pruning
b. Connectionist expert systems
c. Pay Band
d. Continuous

14. _____ has been described as the 'process of social influence in which one person can enlist the aid and support of others in the accomplishment of a common task'. A definition more inclusive of followers comes from Alan Keith of Genentech who said '_____ is ultimately about creating a way for people to contribute to making something extraordinary happen.'

_____ is one of the most salient aspects of the organizational context. However, defining _____ has been challenging.

a. Situational leadership
b. 28-hour day
c. Leadership
d. 1990 Clean Air Act

15. _____ is an idea in the field of Organizational studies and management which describes the psychology, attitudes, experiences, beliefs and Values (personal and cultural values) of an organization. It has been defined as 'the specific collection of values and norms that are shared by people and groups in an organization and that control the way they interact with each other and with stakeholders outside the organization.'

This definition continues to explain organizational values also known as 'beliefs and ideas about what kinds of goals members of an organization should pursue and ideas about the appropriate kinds or standards of behavior organizational members should use to achieve these goals. From organizational values develop organizational norms, guidelines or expectations that prescribe appropriate kinds of behavior by employees in particular situations and control the behavior of organizational members towards one another.'

_____ is not the same as corporate culture.

a. Organizational effectiveness
b. Union shop
c. Organizational development
d. Organizational culture

16. _____ consists of the mental process of thinking involved with the process of judging the merits of multiple options and selecting one of them for action. Some simple examples include deciding whether to get up in the morning or go back to sleep, or selecting a given route for a journey. More complex examples (often decisions that affect what a person thinks or their core beliefs) include choosing a lifestyle, religious affiliation, or political position.

a. Groups decision making
b. Championship mobilization
c. Choice
d. Trade study

Chapter 25. Quality Assurance and Improvement

17. _____, a business term, is a measure of how products and services supplied by a company meet or surpass customer expectation. It is seen as a key performance indicator within business and is part of the four perspectives of a Balanced Scorecard.

In a competitive marketplace where businesses compete for customers, _____ is seen as a key differentiator and increasingly has become a key element of business strategy.

a. Customer satisfaction
b. Foreign ownership
c. Critical Success Factor
d. Horizontal integration

18. _____ is a statistical technique in decision making that is used for selection of a limited number of tasks that produce significant overall effect. It uses the Pareto principle - the idea that by doing 20% of work you can generate 80% of the advantage of doing the entire job. Or in terms of quality improvement, a large majority of problems (80%) are produced by a few key causes (20%.)

a. Goodness of fit
b. Polychoric correlation
c. Probability matching
d. Pareto analysis

19. In statistics, a _____ is a graphical display of tabulated frequencies, shown as bars. It shows what proportion of cases fall into each of several categories: it is a form of data binning. The categories are usually specified as non-overlapping intervals of some variable.

a. Statistics
b. Standard deviation
c. Correlation
d. Histogram

20. The _____ in statistical process control is a tool used to determine whether a manufacturing or business process is in a state of statistical control or not.

If the chart indicates that the process is currently under control then it can be used with confidence to predict the future performance of the process. If the chart indicates that the process being monitored is not in control, the pattern it reveals can help determine the source of variation to be eliminated to bring the process back into control.

a. Time series analysis
b. Failure rate
c. Simple moving average
d. Control chart

21. A _____ is a common type of chart, that represents an algorithm or process, showing the steps as boxes of various kinds, and their order by connecting these with arrows. _____s are used in analyzing, designing, documenting or managing a process or program in various fields.

The first structured method for documenting process flow, the 'flow process chart', was introduced by Frank Gilbreth to members of ASME in 1921 as the presentation 'Process Charts--First Steps in Finding the One Best Way'.

a. Flowchart
b. 33 Strategies of War
c. 28-hour day
d. 1990 Clean Air Act

Chapter 26. Physician Practice: Organization and Operation

1. A _____ is a type of bar chart that illustrates a project schedule. _____s illustrate the start and finish dates of the terminal elements and summary elements of a project. Terminal elements and summary elements comprise the work breakdown structure of the project.

    a. 1990 Clean Air Act
    b. 33 Strategies of War
    c. 28-hour day
    d. Gantt chart

2. _____ refers to the process of screening, and selecting qualified people for a job at an organization or firm mid- and large-size organizations and companies often retain professional recruiters or outsource some of the process to _____ agencies. External _____ is the process of attracting and selecting employees from outside the organization.

    The _____ industry has four main types of agencies: employment agencies, _____ websites and job search engines, 'headhunters' for executive and professional _____, and in-house _____.

    a. Referral recruitment
    b. Recruitment
    c. Labour hire
    d. Recruitment Process Outsourcing

3. _____ is an advertisement in which a particular product specifically mentions a competitor by name for the express purpose of showing why the competitor is inferior to the product naming it.

    This should not be confused with parody advertisements, where a fictional product is being advertised for the purpose of poking fun at the particular advertisement, nor should it be confused with the use of a coined brand name for the purpose of comparing the product without actually naming an actual competitor. ('Wikipedia tastes better and is less filling than the Encyclopedia Galactica.')

    In the 1980s, during what has been referred to as the cola wars, soft-drink manufacturer Pepsi ran a series of advertisements where people, caught on hidden camera, in a blind taste test, chose Pepsi over rival Coca-Cola.

    a. 28-hour day
    b. 1990 Clean Air Act
    c. 33 Strategies of War
    d. Comparative advertising

4. In economics, business, retail, and accounting, a _____ is the value of money that has been used up to produce something, and hence is not available for use anymore. In economics, a _____ is an alternative that is given up as a result of a decision. In business, the _____ may be one of acquisition, in which case the amount of money expended to acquire it is counted as _____.

    a. Fixed costs
    b. Cost overrun
    c. Cost allocation
    d. Cost

5. _____ is the process of comparing the cost, cycle time, productivity, or quality of a specific process or method to another that is widely considered to be an industry standard or best practice. Essentially, _____ provides a snapshot of the performance of your business and helps you understand where you are in relation to a particular standard. The result is often a business case for making changes in order to make improvements.

    a. Benchmarking
    b. Cost leadership
    c. Complementors
    d. Competitive heterogeneity

Chapter 26. Physician Practice: Organization and Operation

6. A _____ is the belief that there is a technique, method, process, activity, incentive or reward that is more effective at delivering a particular outcome than any other technique, method, process, etc. The idea is that with proper processes, checks, and testing, a desired outcome can be delivered with fewer problems and unforeseen complications. _____s can also be defined as the most efficient (least amount of effort) and effective (best results) way of accomplishing a task, based on repeatable procedures that have proven themselves over time for large numbers of people.

   a. Hierarchical organization
   b. Design management
   c. Fix it twice
   d. Best practice

7. Market _____ is a business, economics or investment term that refers to an asset's ability to be easily converted through an act of buying or selling without causing a significant movement in the price and with minimum loss of value. Money, or cash on hand, is the most liquid asset. An act of exchange of a less liquid asset with a more liquid asset is called liquidation.

   a. 1990 Clean Air Act
   b. 28-hour day
   c. 33 Strategies of War
   d. Liquidity

8. _____ is one of a series of accounting transactions dealing with the billing of customers who owe money to a person, company or organization for goods and services that have been provided to the customer. In most business entities this is typically done by generating an invoice and mailing or electronically delivering it to the customer, who in turn must pay it within an established timeframe called credit or payment terms.

An example of a common payment term is Net 30, meaning payment is due in the amount of the invoice 30 days from the date of invoice.

   a. Other revenue
   b. A Stake in the Outcome
   c. Accumulated Depreciation
   d. Accounts receivable

Chapter 27. Implementing a Physician Practice Compliance Program

1. A _____ is a type of bar chart that illustrates a project schedule. _____s illustrate the start and finish dates of the terminal elements and summary elements of a project. Terminal elements and summary elements comprise the work breakdown structure of the project.
   a. 1990 Clean Air Act
   b. 28-hour day
   c. Gantt chart
   d. 33 Strategies of War

2. The general definition of an _____ is an evaluation of a person, organization, system, process, project or product. _____s are performed to ascertain the validity and reliability of information; also to provide an assessment of a system's internal control. The goal of an _____ is to express an opinion on the person / organization/system (etc) in question, under evaluation based on work done on a test basis.
   a. Audit committee
   b. A Stake in the Outcome
   c. Internal control
   d. Audit

3. A _____ is a list of the general tasks and responsibilities of a position. Typically, it also includes to whom the position reports, specifications such as the qualifications needed by the person in the job, salary range for the position, etc. A _____ is usually developed by conducting a job analysis, which includes examining the tasks and sequences of tasks necessary to perform the job.
   a. Recruitment Process Insourcing
   b. Job description
   c. Recruitment
   d. Recruitment advertising

4. _____ describes the situation when output from (or information about the result of) an event or phenomenon in the past will influence the same event/phenomenon in the present or future. When an event is part of a chain of cause-and-effect that forms a circuit or loop, then the event is said to 'feed back' into itself.

   _____ is also a synonym for:

   - _____ signal; the information about the initial event that is the basis for subsequent modification of the event.
   - _____ loop; the causal path that leads from the initial generation of the _____ signal to the subsequent modification of the event.

   _____ is a mechanism, process or signal that is looped back to control a system within itself. Such a loop is called a _____ loop.

   a. 1990 Clean Air Act
   b. Positive feedback
   c. Feedback loop
   d. Feedback

5. _____ is an increasingly broadening term with which an organization, or other human system describes the combination of traditionally administrative personnel functions with acquisition and application of skills, knowledge and experience, Employee Relations and resource planning at various levels. The field draws upon concepts developed in Industrial/Organizational Psychology and System Theory. _____ has at least two related interpretations depending on context. The original usage derives from political economy and economics, where it was traditionally called labor, one of four factors of production although this perspective is changing as a function of new and ongoing research into more strategic approaches at national levels. This first usage is used more in terms of '_____ development', and can go beyond just organizations to the level of nations. The more traditional usage within corporations and businesses refers to the individuals within a firm or agency, and to the portion of the organization that deals with hiring, firing, training, and other personnel issues, typically referred to as '_____ management'.

Chapter 27. Implementing a Physician Practice Compliance Program

a. Human resource management
b. Progressive discipline
c. Bradford Factor
d. Human resources

6. Organizational culture is not the same as _____. It is wider and deeper concepts, something that an organization 'is' rather than what it 'has' (according to Buchanan and Huczynski.)

_____ is the total sum of the values, customs, traditions and meanings that make a company unique.

a. Work design
b. Job analysis
c. Path-goal theory
d. Corporate culture

7. Various _____ can be employed dependent on the culture of the business, the nature of the task, the nature of the workforce and the personality and skills of the leaders. This idea was further developed by Robert Tannenbaum and Warren H. Schmidt (1958, 1973) who argued that the style of leadership is dependent upon the prevailing circumstance; therefore leaders should exercise a range of leadership styles and should deploy them as appropriate.

An Autocratic or authoritarian manager makes all the decisions, keeping the information and decision making among the senior management.

a. 1990 Clean Air Act
b. 28-hour day
c. 33 Strategies of War
d. Management styles

8. _____, widely known as F. W. Taylor, was an American mechanical engineer who sought to improve industrial efficiency. He is regarded as the father of scientific management, and was one of the first management consultants.

Taylor was one of the intellectual leaders of the Efficiency Movement and his ideas, broadly conceived, were highly influential in the Progressive Era.

a. Douglas N. Daft
b. Jonah Jacob Goldberg
c. Geoffrey Colvin
d. Frederick Winslow Taylor

9. A _____ is a change implemented to address a weakness identified in a management system. Normally _____s are implemented in response to a customer complaint, abnormal levels of internal nonconformity, nonconformities identified during an internal audit or adverse or unstable trends in product and process monitoring such as would be identified by SPC.

The process of determining a _____ requires identification of actions that can be taken to prevent or mitigate the weakness.

a. 1990 Clean Air Act
b. Corrective action
c. 28-hour day
d. Zero defects

10. A _____ is a brief written statement of the purpose of a company or organization. Ideally, a _____ guides the actions of the organization, spells out its overall goal, provides a sense of direction, and guides decision making for all levels of management.

Chapter 27. Implementing a Physician Practice Compliance Program

_____s often contain the following:

- Purpose and aim of the organization
- The organization's primary stakeholders: clients, stockholders, etc.
- Responsibilities of the organization toward these stakeholders
- Products and services offered

In developing a _____:

- Encourage as much input as feasible from employees, volunteers, and other stakeholders
- Publicize it broadly

The _____ can be used to resolve differences between business stakeholders. Stakeholders include: employees including managers and executives, stockholders, board of directors, customers, suppliers, distributors, creditors, governments (local, state, federal, etc.), unions, competitors, NGO's, and the general public.

a. 1990 Clean Air Act
b. 28-hour day
c. 33 Strategies of War
d. Mission statement

11. A _____ is a body of elected or appointed members who jointly oversee the activities of a company or organization. The body sometimes has a different name, such as board of trustees, board of governors, board of managers, or executive board. It is often simply referred to as 'the board.'

A board's activities are determined by the powers, duties, and responsibilities delegated to it or conferred on it by an authority outside itself.

a. Foreign Corrupt Practices Act
b. Board of directors
c. Clean Water Act
d. Competition law

12. A mutual _____ or stockholder is an individual or company (including a corporation) that legally owns one or more shares of stock in a joint stock company. A company's _____s collectively own that company. Thus, the typical goal of such companies is to enhance _____ value.

a. Shareholder
b. 1990 Clean Air Act
c. Stockholder
d. Free riding

13. _____ refers to the process of screening, and selecting qualified people for a job at an organization or firm mid- and large-size organizations and companies often retain professional recruiters or outsource some of the process to _____ agencies. External _____ is the process of attracting and selecting employees from outside the organization.

The _____ industry has four main types of agencies: employment agencies, _____ websites and job search engines, 'headhunters' for executive and professional _____, and in-house _____.

a. Recruitment Process Outsourcing
c. Labour hire
b. Referral recruitment
d. Recruitment

14. In decision theory and estimation theory, the _____ of an estimator, $\hat{\theta}$, of an unknown parameter of the distribution, θ, is the expected value of the loss function

$$R(\theta, \hat{\theta}) = \mathbb{E}_\theta L(\theta, \hat{\theta}) = \int L(\theta, \hat{\theta})\, dP_\theta.$$

where dP_θ is a probability measure parametrized by θ.

- For a scalar parameter θ and a quadratic loss function,

$$L(\theta, \hat{\theta}) = (\theta - \hat{\theta})^2$$

the _____ function becomes the mean squared error of the estimate,

$$R(\theta, \hat{\theta}) = E_\theta (\theta - \hat{\theta})^2$$

- In density estimation, the unknown parameter is probability density itself. The loss function is typically chosen to be a norm in an appropriate function space. For example, for L^2 norm,

$$L(f, \hat{f}) = \|f - \hat{f}\|_2^2$$

the _____ function becomes the mean integrated squared error

$$R(f, \hat{f}) = E\|f - \hat{f}\|^2$$

a. Risk
c. Financial modeling
b. Risk aversion
d. Linear model

15. _____ is a step in a risk management process. _____ is the determination of quantitative or qualitative value of risk related to a concrete situation and a recognized threat (also called hazard.) Quantitative _____ requires calculations of two components of risk: R, the magnitude of the potential loss L, and the probability p, that the loss will occur.
  a. 1990 Clean Air Act
  c. Quality assurance
  b. 28-hour day
  d. Risk assessment

Chapter 1
1. b   2. d   3. b   4. d   5. d   6. c   7. a   8. c   9. c   10. c
11. d   12. d   13. d

Chapter 2
1. d   2. d   3. b   4. a   5. a   6. b   7. d   8. d   9. c   10. c
11. b   12. d   13. d   14. d   15. a   16. d   17. d   18. d   19. d   20. a
21. c   22. c   23. b   24. d   25. d   26. d   27. a   28. b   29. a

Chapter 3
1. c   2. b   3. d   4. b   5. d   6. d   7. d   8. d   9. c   10. a
11. d   12. d   13. d   14. c   15. d   16. c   17. a   18. d

Chapter 4
1. b   2. d   3. d   4. d   5. b   6. d   7. b   8. b   9. b   10. d
11. a   12. d   13. b   14. b   15. d

Chapter 5
1. d   2. c   3. d   4. a   5. b   6. d   7. a   8. a   9. d   10. a
11. a   12. a   13. d   14. b   15. c   16. d   17. d   18. b   19. d   20. d
21. b   22. d   23. d   24. c   25. d   26. d   27. d   28. a   29. d   30. c
31. d   32. d   33. d   34. d   35. a   36. d   37. c   38. d   39. d   40. c
41. d   42. d   43. d   44. d   45. d   46. d   47. d   48. b   49. b   50. a
51. b   52. d   53. d   54. d   55. d   56. d   57. c   58. a

Chapter 6
1. d   2. a   3. d   4. c   5. b   6. d   7. d   8. c   9. d   10. d
11. c   12. c   13. c   14. d   15. b   16. d   17. d   18. d   19. b   20. d
21. a   22. b   23. d   24. a   25. d   26. c   27. d   28. a   29. b   30. d
31. b   32. d   33. b   34. a   35. d   36. d   37. d   38. d   39. b

Chapter 7
1. a   2. d   3. d   4. d   5. a   6. a   7. a   8. a   9. a   10. d
11. d   12. b   13. d   14. b   15. b   16. b   17. d   18. d   19. d   20. a
21. a   22. d   23. d   24. a   25. d   26. a   27. b   28. d   29. c   30. d
31. a   32. a   33. c   34. d   35. b   36. d   37. b   38. d   39. b   40. a
41. d   42. d   43. b   44. d   45. c   46. d   47. a   48. d   49. b

Chapter 8
1. a   2. b   3. d   4. b   5. d   6. d   7. b   8. d   9. d

Chapter 9
1. c   2. d   3. c   4. d   5. c   6. d   7. d   8. d   9. b   10. c
11. b   12. b

ANSWER KEY

Chapter 10
1. d   2. a   3. d   4. d   5. d   6. d   7. d   8. b   9. c   10. d
11. d   12. a   13. a   14. c   15. d   16. c   17. b   18. c   19. c   20. d
21. d   22. d

Chapter 11
1. d   2. a   3. a   4. d   5. d   6. d   7. d   8. d   9. a   10. b
11. d   12. b   13. c   14. a   15. c   16. d   17. d   18. a

Chapter 12
1. b   2. d   3. d   4. d   5. c   6. a   7. c   8. a

Chapter 13
1. d   2. d   3. d   4. d   5. d   6. d   7. b   8. b   9. d   10. a
11. a   12. b   13. d   14. d   15. a   16. b   17. d   18. d

Chapter 14
1. d   2. a   3. d   4. d   5. d   6. d   7. d   8. d   9. d   10. d
11. c

Chapter 15
1. b   2. c   3. d   4. d   5. c   6. d   7. a   8. d   9. b   10. d
11. b   12. b   13. a   14. d   15. d   16. b   17. b   18. c   19. d   20. d

Chapter 16
1. c   2. d   3. a   4. d   5. a   6. c

Chapter 17
1. d   2. d

Chapter 18
1. d   2. d   3. d   4. b   5. d   6. d

Chapter 19
1. b   2. b   3. a   4. b   5. d   6. a   7. d   8. c   9. d   10. b
11. d

Chapter 20
1. a   2. c   3. d   4. b   5. c   6. b   7. c   8. c   9. d   10. d

Chapter 21
1. d   2. d   3. a   4. a   5. d   6. b   7. b   8. b   9. c   10. b
11. d   12. d

Chapter 22
   1. d   2. d   3. d   4. a   5. d   6. a   7. b   8. d   9. a   10. c
   11. d   12. c   13. c   14. d   15. d   16. b

Chapter 23
   1. a   2. b   3. d   4. d   5. d   6. b   7. d   8. a   9. a   10. d
   11. d   12. a   13. b

Chapter 24
   1. a   2. d   3. c   4. a   5. d   6. d   7. d   8. c   9. b   10. a
   11. d   12. d

Chapter 25
   1. d   2. c   3. c   4. d   5. d   6. a   7. b   8. d   9. d   10. a
   11. d   12. b   13. d   14. c   15. d   16. c   17. a   18. d   19. d   20. d
   21. a

Chapter 26
   1. d   2. b   3. d   4. d   5. a   6. d   7. d   8. d

Chapter 27
   1. c   2. d   3. b   4. d   5. d   6. d   7. d   8. d   9. b   10. d
   11. b   12. a   13. d   14. a   15. d

www.ingramcontent.com/pod-product-compliance
Lightning Source LLC
Chambersburg PA
CBHW082049230426
43670CB00016B/2831